DrawPj.com

12 Charcoal Techniques

The Complete Five Week Course

With Author/Illustrator Cindy Wider

Contents

General overview of this course

This five week complete course in charcoal presents to you all the basic techniques that you need to create realistic drawings in charcoal. It is divided into a series of exercises separated into five separate weeks of study. This is to help you complete your course by studying for a couple of hours a week on a regular basis. It is highly recommended that you work consistently to develop your charcoal drawing skills to the fullest. If you need more help in learning to draw and shade you might consider studying the 'complete drawing and painting certificate course' by Cindy Wider.

Course Outline:

Week One

- Introduction to week one

- Introduction to charcoal

- Pre-instruction drawing

- Learn twelve charcoal techniques allowing you to create hundreds of textures

Week Two

- Learn to draw hair with three different hairstyles presented, using charcoal and white conte on grey paper

Week Three

- Draw a variety of objects using charcoal with white conte on grey Mi-Teintes paper using the construction drawing method

Weeks Four and Five

- Begin your project: Take a photograph of yourself and use the step-by-step process to draw your own self-portrait or draw the image provided. female face. To draw yourself is the most ideal as often you will want to see parts of your face that may not be clearly understood in the photograph due to missing information. Your portrait will be drawn on the smooth side of grey Mi-Teintes paper using charcoal and white conte.

Week One

Introduction to week one

During this first week of your course, you will be asked to create a pre-instruction drawing. Then you will be introduced to the incredible possibilities of charcoal. You will be shown how to use both willow stick and pencil charcoal with an eraser and white Conté on grey Mi-Teintes paper to create twelve different effects. After this week you will be fully aware of the wonderful qualities of charcoal and the huge array of possible results that can be achieved with this amazing medium. Make sure you read all of your notes before beginning the exercises.

Create a pre-instruction drawing

It is important that you record your current drawing ability in a pre-instruction drawing so that at the end of the course, we can look back to see how much you have improved. Please draw a picture of your face using a mirror *(not a photograph).*

There are no expectations of you whatsoever and if you see the examples below of some typical beginner self-portraits you will notice that people come into this course at all levels of ability. If you are an absolute beginner, this picture you create will probably be the same as your ability when you were about a twelve year old child. Treat this light-heartedly. It's fun and try to have no expectations whatsoever!

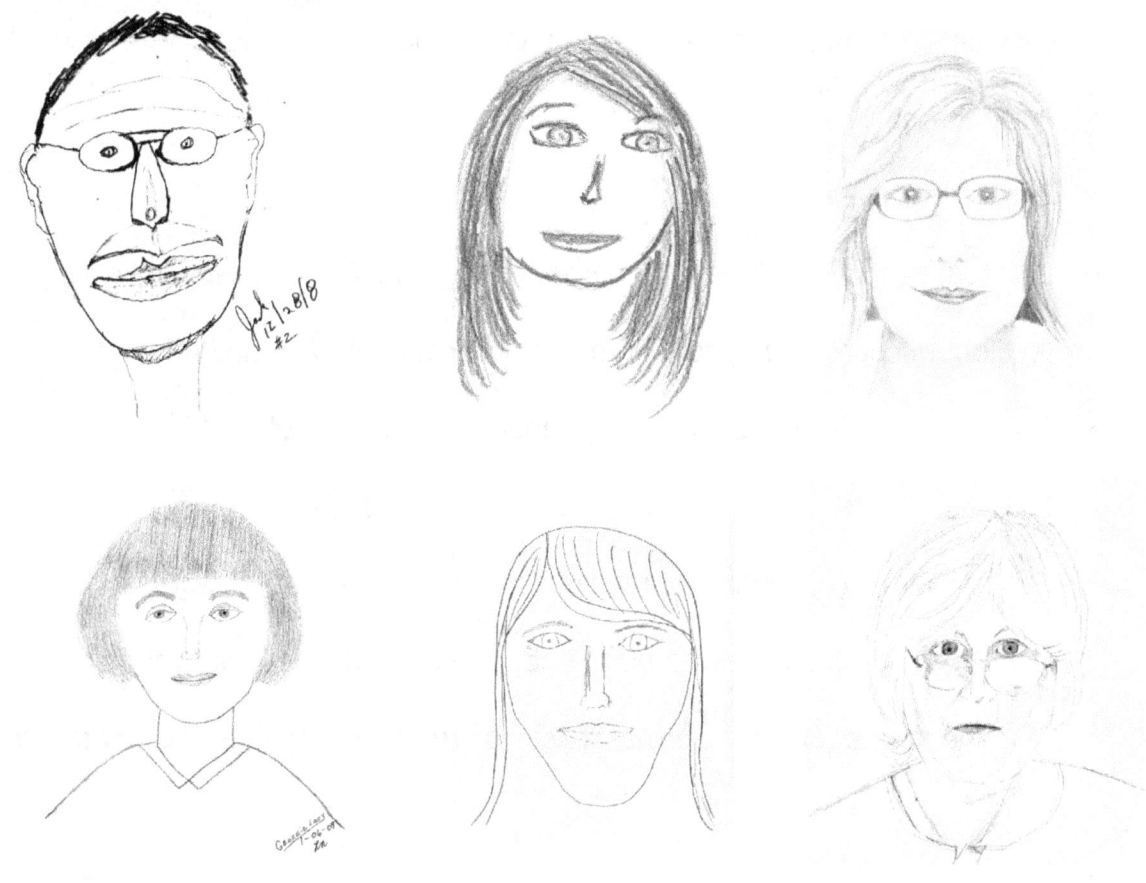

www.DrawPJ.com

Introduction to Charcoal

Charcoal has been used in various forms by artists for centuries and is one of the oldest drawing materials. The Charcoal that artists use these days is made from willow, a plant that grows in long rods up to seven feet high. Willow is grown in plantations and harvested every year in winter. The willow is cut into long lengths, bundled up and boiled in water. It is cleaned, dried in open air then sawn to the right length before being placed in metal boxes, filled with sand and lids placed on. The sticks are then fired at a very high temperature in a kiln for several hours before being left to cool. The entire process takes about three days. Finally the sticks are packaged and sent off to stores.

Art materials used for charcoal drawing

Here are a list of art materials needed to complete this course. Refer to the list below and the photograph (see Figs. 1a and 1b) of the materials that you will be using (apart from the fixative which comes in many brands.)

- HB Charcoal Pencil (for fine lines)

- White charcoal pencil or white conte stick

- Several Willow charcoal sticks preferably 6mm and 9mm in diameter

- Click eraser or normal plastic eraser and craft knife to cut the tip

- Putty Eraser (or kneaded eraser)

- Ruler (clear plastic)

- Charcoal Pencil Sharpener (normal sharpener can shatter charcoal pencil)

- Medium to coarse sandpaper 80 grit (to prepare willow charcoal)

- Paper: Canson Mi-Teintes Drawing Paper – light grey (colour 122)

- Soft, clean water colour brush (for dusting your page)

- Can of fixative (optional to spray your charcoal drawing afterwards)

- Non-greasy baking paper (to place under your hand while you work)

- Glassine sheets (Optional, protects your drawing. Buy from art supply stores.)

Charcoal papers

The type of paper you choose for charcoal drawing is a vitally important part of the process of drawing with charcoal. Charcoal cannot adhere to a glossy or shiny surface. The paper needs to have a little bit of texture, or 'tooth.'

There are many different papers on the market which you can use, with a variety of colours. Many artists use the paper I have suggested in your course notes; Canson Mi-Teintes paper. This paper which has a 65% rag content is very strong. It is especially designed to allow repeated reworking so it is ideal for charcoal work.

One side of this paper is smooth and the other is quite textured; both sides give different effects. You are asked to purchase a mid-toned (light) grey paper so the colour of the paper can then double as the middle value tones in your artwork. It gives your drawing a fresh appearance if leave the paper untouched in those areas.

Your choice of paper is really just a matter of personal preference, providing you choose a paper with some tooth. Watercolour papers are also great to use. You can use white paper with charcoal, however for the purpose of this course your will need to use grey paper with a little tooth.

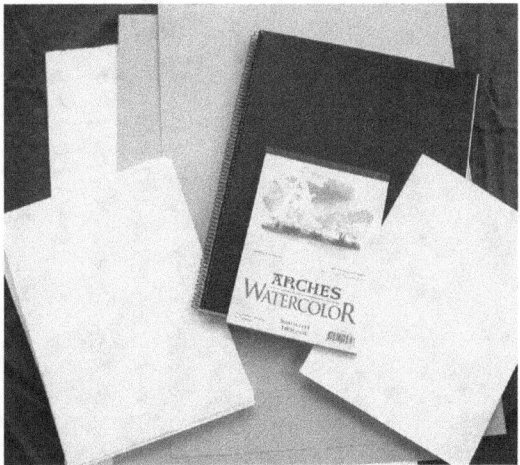

Fig. 1a. A selection of papers from your list of supplies

Fixing your image after completion

Charcoal images are very delicate as the particles can easily fall off the surface of the paper. To protect your image from smudging with a swipe of your finger, you can spray your artwork with a 'Fixative.' There are some very good spray fixatives available on the market today. When sprayed your image usually dries very similar to before you sprayed, or it may go a little darker. Always test a small sample whenever using any new product to see the effect before using it on an important artwork. Spraying your charcoal drawings still does not completely protect your work but just makes it a little less likely to smudge.

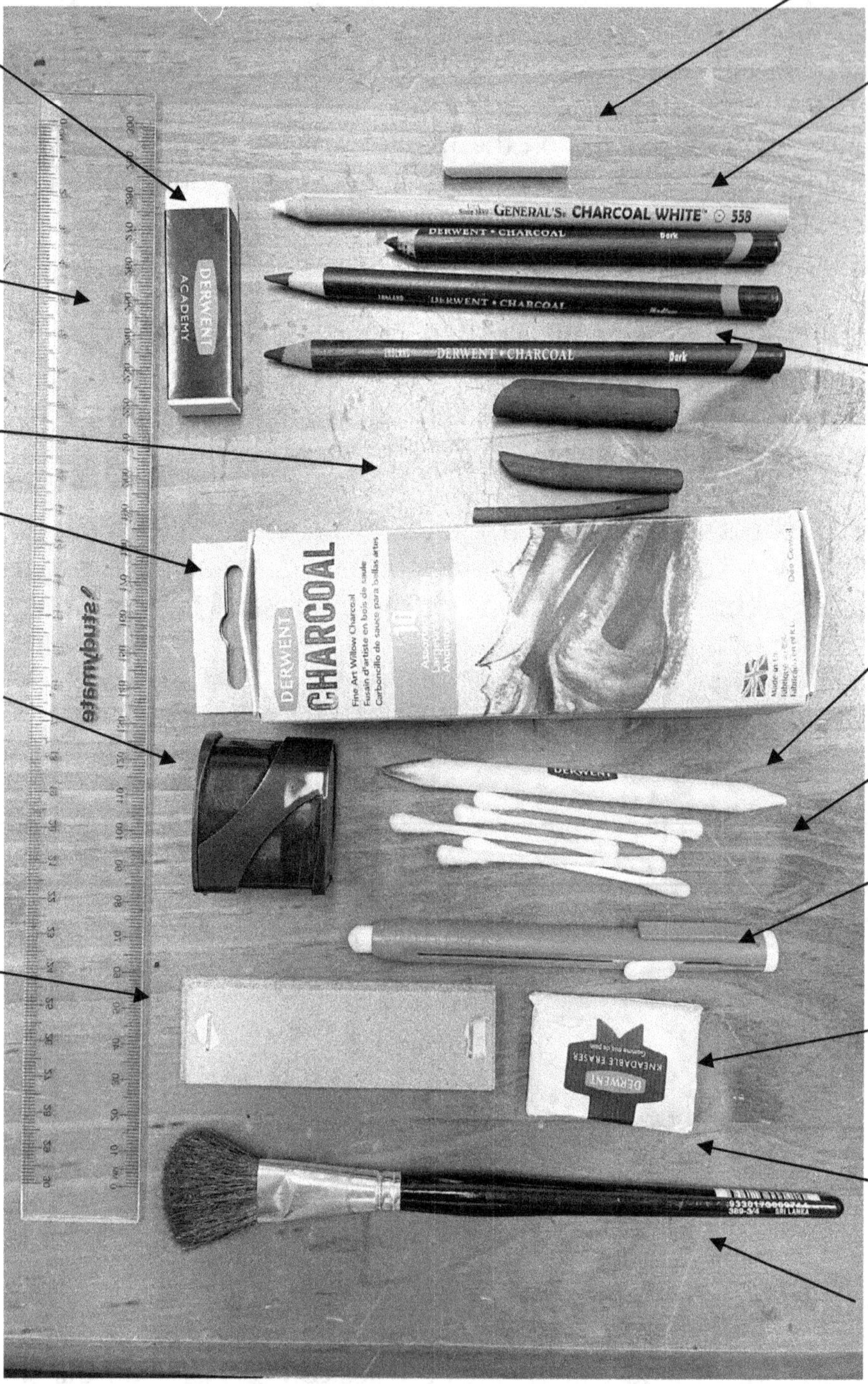

Plastic Eraser. You can cut this to a sharp edge or use a click-eraser cut to a 'V' or chisel point on the tip

Clear ruler

Sticks of Willow Charcoal and a box of three sizes approx.. 14mm, 9mm and 6mm or similar sizes.

Sharpener for charcoal pencils

Sandpaper. This small sheet of sandpaper is for the charcoal pencils you also need to use a more coarse 80 grit andpaper for willow charcoal stick.

Gum eraser (not in the image and optional)

White conte

White charcoal pencil

2B and HB or Dark and Medium charcoal pencils for fine lines

Paper stump small and large

Cotton buds or Q-tips

Pen Eraser

Putty eraser with a small ball rolled ready to use.

Soft water-colour brush to wipe away erasings; brush above - without touching the paper.

Fig. 1b. Materials from your list of supplies

Willow charcoal and charcoal pencils

During this course we will be using charcoal that has been prepared by the manufacturer in two different ways; willow charcoal sticks and charcoal pencils. Charcoal pencils are quite difficult to erase. We will mostly be using these for fine details or after an initial under-drawing with the willow charcoal stick. We have two of each the HB and 2B.

There are three sizes of willow charcoal that we will be using in this unit of the course; thick (14mm in diameter), medium (9mm in diameter) and thin (6mm in diameter.) Providing you don't press too hard, willow charcoal will wipe off your paper almost like chalk off a blackboard. Just a fine line will be left behind. Often called a 'Ghost line,' this remaining fine line that cannot be removed becomes an expressive part of your drawing.

You will be shown how to prepare your willow charcoal so that you can achieve either very fine lines or cover large areas.

Tip: Never use graphite pencil with charcoal unless you are absolutely sure where you are placing the graphite. Charcoal cannot easily be placed over the top of an area of graphite as it repels the charcoal. During this course we will not be using and graphite whatsoever.

Loose charcoal powder

Loose charcoal powder can be purchased from some art supply stores or over the internet, however, you will soon find that you create plenty of this powder while preparing your willow sticks for use. All three willow sticks; thick, medium and thin, can be shaved across the coarse sandpaper (80 grit size) to create a tip ready for drawing with. This process is described in detail shortly (see Fig. 3a.)

If you hold the sandpaper facing downwards over a small container and tap or flick the back of it with your index finger and thumb, the powder will fall out of the sandpaper into the container. This also cleans your sandpaper at the same time as providing you with lots of loose powder for future use.

Exercise for week one: Twelve charcoal techniques

In this exercise you will be asked to create twelve different charcoal techniques on one single sheet of Mi-Teintes grey paper. Make sure you have all of your charcoal equipment ready for use before you begin.

You will be asked to experiment on both the smooth and the rough side of this paper, however for your final scanned image, please create your techniques on the **smooth side** for your exercises.

Prepare your paper

Before you begin this exercise, make sure you have your sheet of Mi-Teintes paper with the **smooth side facing upwards**. Rule this sheet of paper into twelve similar-sized sections using a ruler and HB Charcoal pencil. You can do this simply by approximation like this;

1. Divide your page into three roughly-even sections vertically. Use your ruler and a HB charcoal pencil for neatness but no need to measure.
2. Turn your page sideways and divide it into quarters horizontally.

You can be creative with the small patterns that you create in each section. You don't have to copy the same shapes in the designs that are demonstrated. Have some fun with the following charcoal techniques. Write these names of each technique in a box before you place an example in the individual sections so that you have a reference to use for all of your future charcoal work;

1. **Cover large areas with willow charcoal**
2. **Cover medium-sized areas with willow charcoal**
3. **Cover small areas with charcoal powder and a stump**
4. **Draw fine lines with willow charcoal**
5. **Draw fine lines with charcoal pencil**
6. **Create gradations with blending**
7. **Create soft edges with blending**
8. **Create hard edges**
9. **Hatching lines with willow charcoal and charcoal pencil**
10. **Lines with variations in widths**
11. **Erasing techniques**
12. **White conte and white charcoal techniques**

1. Cover large areas with willow charcoal

You can cover a large area of your paper in several ways. In this first technique you will be learning the method of laying a thick piece of willow charcoal on its side and dragging it across the surface. Please create the following technique in the first box on your sheet of Mi-Teintes paper;

1. Begin by breaking a thick willow stick into thirds or a half.
2. Lay this piece of charcoal on its side and drag it back and forth across the surface of ***coarse sandpaper*** a couple of times to create a flat edge.
3. Place this piece of charcoal onto your Mi-Teintes paper (see Fig. 2a) with the flat side touching the page then rub or drag it across the surface. You can do this in any direction as well as vary the pressure. Try some wavy, circular, horizontal, vertical or diagonal strokes.
4. Try this first stoke on the smooth side (see Fig. 2b) of your paper and then on the rough side (see Fig. 2c.) You will notice the pattern of the paper appear more obviously on the rough side. For the purpose of sending your work in for comment, please just select the smooth side of your paper to scan and send in to your tutor.
5. Depending on the amount of pressure you apply, you can achieve slightly different levels of tone with this technique.

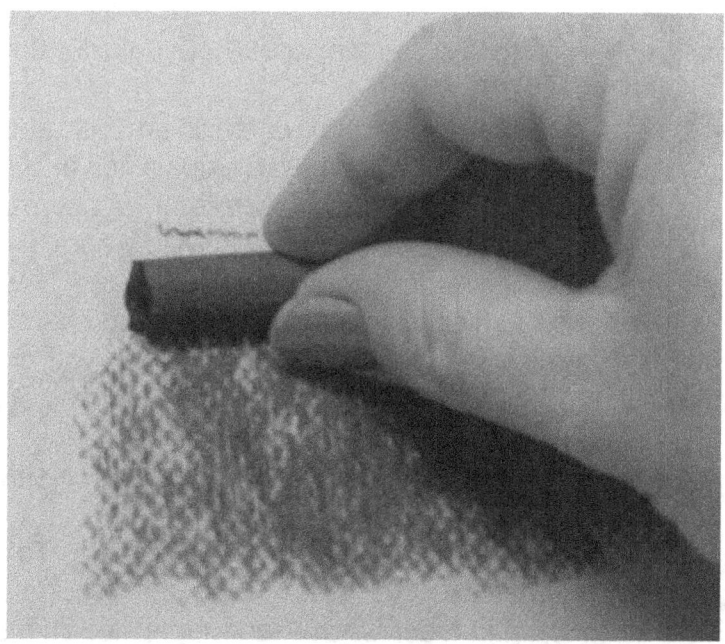

Fig. 2a 14mm Willow Charcoal held on the side

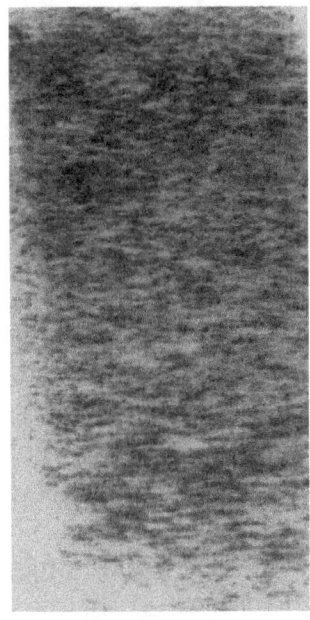
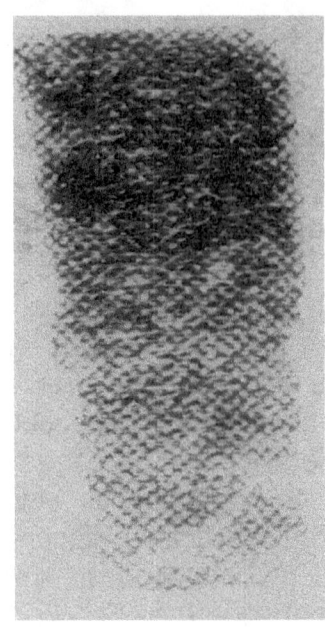

2b. Smooth side of Mi-teintes   Fig. 2c. Textured side of Mi-teintes

2. Cover medium sized areas with willow charcoal

You can cover medium sized areas of your page using either your thick or medium willow charcoal stick prepared in a special way known as the 'Chisel Point' tip.

1. Place a small section of coarse sandpaper (80 grit) onto a flat surface such as a table.
2. Gently rest the tip of your willow charcoal stick on the sandpaper holding it perpendicular to the surface to begin with. Gradually lower the charcoal until it is approximately on a ***30° angle off the surface of the table.*** Holding it in this position, rub back and forth to shave the willow stick (see Fig. 3a.) As a result of shaving the willow stick, you will create loose powder that can be collected as mentioned earlier in the section on 'loose charcoal powder.' This will be used for a later technique. This shaving action will gradually wear the charcoal down to form the vitally important angle known as a 'chisel point' (see Fig. 3b.)
3. If this is done correctly, you should create a large ellipse shape with a tip on the end.
4. Place the large ellipse-shaped area flat onto your page. To do this, you will need to position it so that you are holding it on the exact same angle as you just held it on when shaving it across the sandpaper (ie: on a 30° angle off the surface of your paper.) Once positioned on your paper you can then drag it across the surface in any direction you choose.
5. By varying the pressure you apply to the willow stick you can create a variety of tones. The harder you press the darker the tone. To achieve very light tones, hold your charcoal with a very soft grip and lightly skim the surface of the paper.

Tip: If, during the shaving process, the tip of your charcoal shatters (or when you are drawing) this means you have applied too much pressure. Make sure that you are holding the ellipse area flat onto the page.

Note: You can also cover small areas of your page using the thin willow charcoal stick prepared and applied in the same way as the thick and medium willow sticks (see Figs. 3c and 3d)

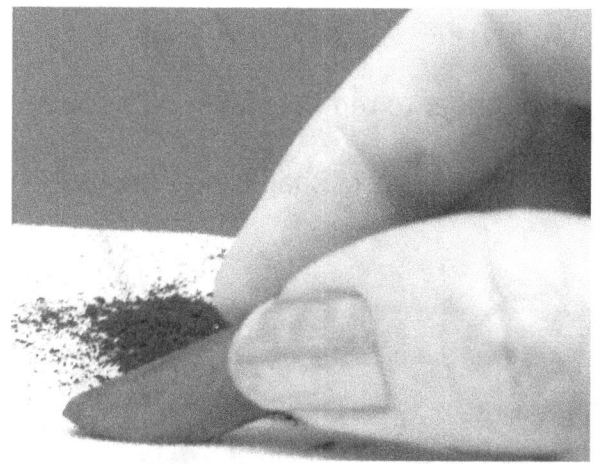

3a. Shave a thick willow on sandpaper

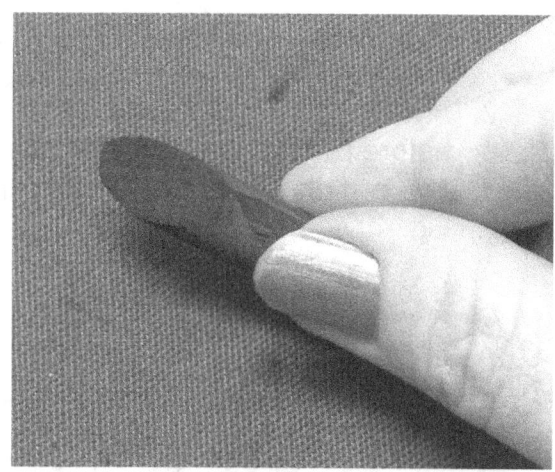

Fig. 3b. Ellipse on thick willow

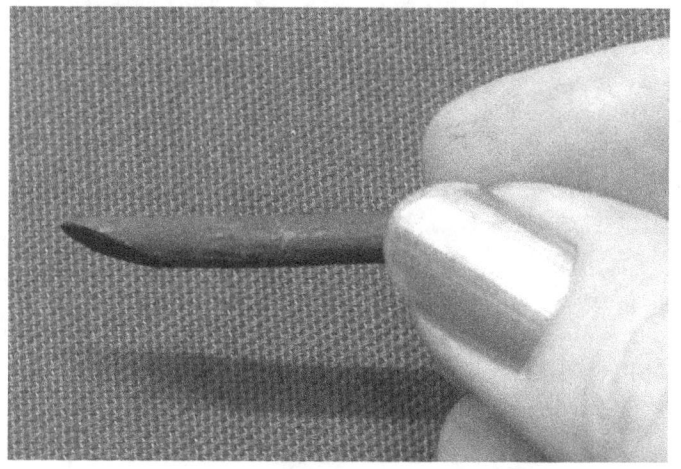

Fig. 3c. Chisel point on thin willow

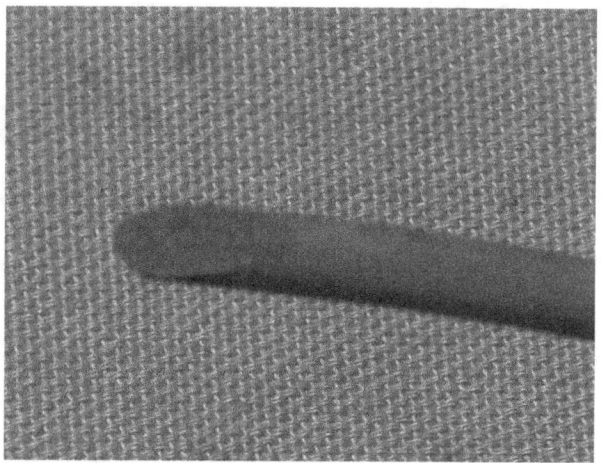

Fig. 3d. Ellipse area on thin willow

3. Cover small areas with willow charcoal powder and a paper stump

If your aim is to achieve a more delicate and lighter tonal area, it is more effective to use just the powder of the charcoal with either a cotton bud (Q-tip) or paper stump (see Fig. 4b.) The difference between using the cotton bud and the paper stump is that the cotton bud doesn't remove as much charcoal as the paper stump does while you blend. The stump is good for creating a neater area and handy for very tiny places. The cotton bud is great for slightly larger areas in which you wish to create a darker level of tone.

For this exercise try both a cotton bud and paper stump to experience the subtle differences. You can be creative with the patterns you make.

1. Gently dip and roll the tip of the paper stump into a small pile of loose charcoal powder (see Fig. 4a.)
2. Always test the stump on a spare sheet of paper to remove the excess powder before beginning your drawing.
3. You can draw with the paper stump making all kinds of shapes and marks (see Fig. 4b.)

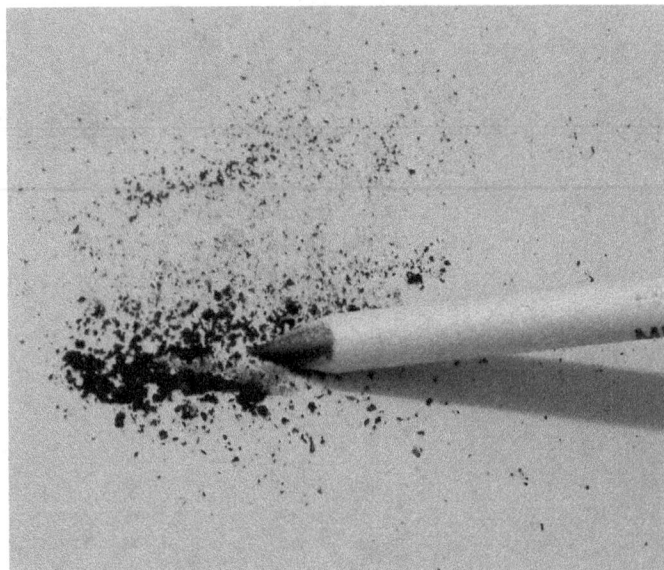 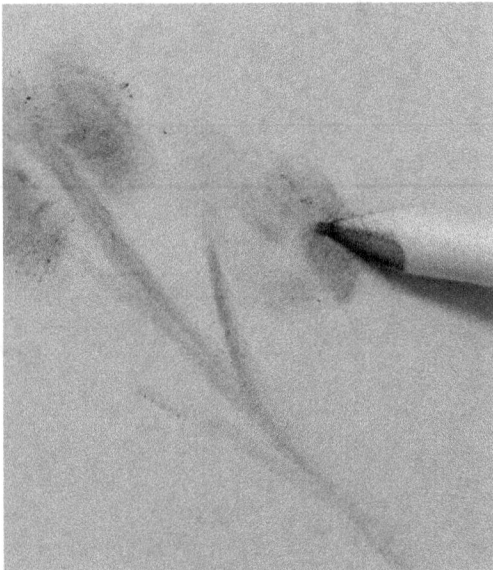

Fig. 4a. Dip the stump into willow powder   Fig. 4b. Draw with the paper stump

4. Draw fine lines with willow charcoal

The chisel-point shape on a stick of willow charcoal also provides us with a thin but strong tip which enables us to create very fine lines. The advantage of being able to use willow charcoal for fine lines is that it is very easy to erase unlike charcoal pencil. It is best to draw your fine lines with willow first then firm these into place with charcoal pencil in any areas you feel a need to darken such as the hair, eyes, nose and lip line. This is not necessary though. You can spray your work once you have completed your drawing to help the charcoal hold in place better.

1. Create some fine lines with your thin willow charcoal stick prepared with a chisel point by placing the narrow tip almost perpendicular to your page (see Fig. 5a.) You can experiment to find the most comfortable position that also allows you to create fine lines.
2. Draw a series of fine lines including straight, wavy and curved strokes (see Fig. 5b.)

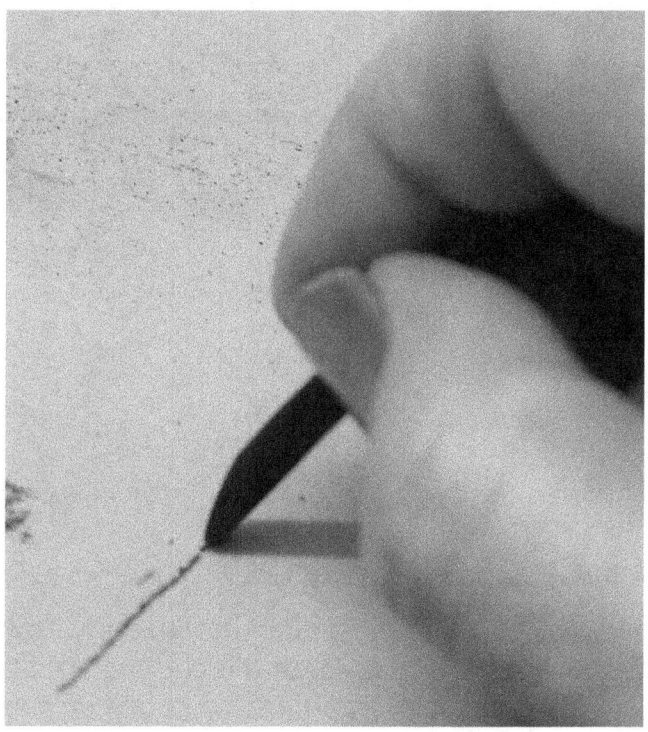
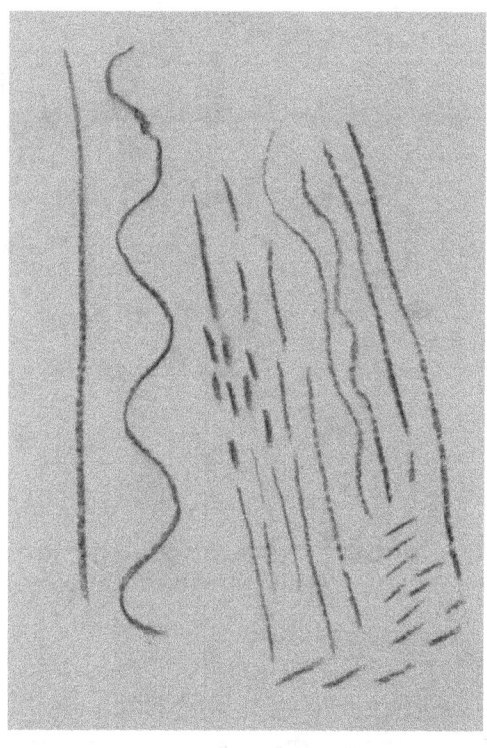

Fig. 5a. Hold the willow stick on its tip   Fig. 5b. Fine lines with willow

5. Draw fine lines with charcoal pencil

We can achieve very fine lines with charcoal pencils. In your collection of art supplies, you should find a HB and 2B *charcoal pencil* as well as a white *charcoal pencil.* The HB is a good pencil for your general drawing of fine details and 2B is a softer pencil which can achieve darker tones. The white charcoal is used to achieve the lightest highlight tones in small areas or thin lines.

Charcoal pencil is quite hard to completely erase so you need to be very sure of your mark-making before applying it to your page. Have a practice with both the black and white charcoal pencils to see the fine lines you can achieve with these (see Figs. 6a and 6b.)

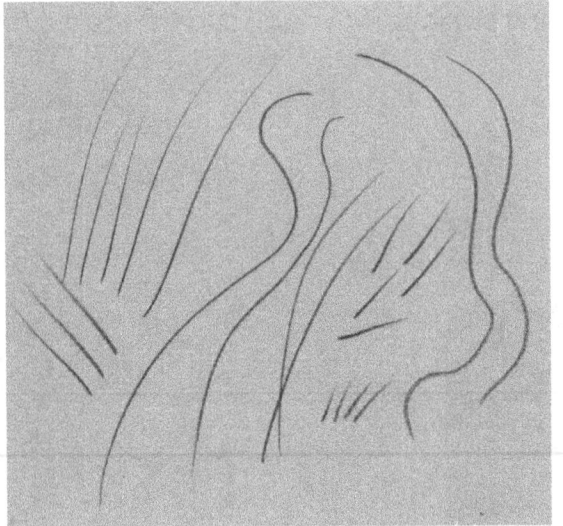
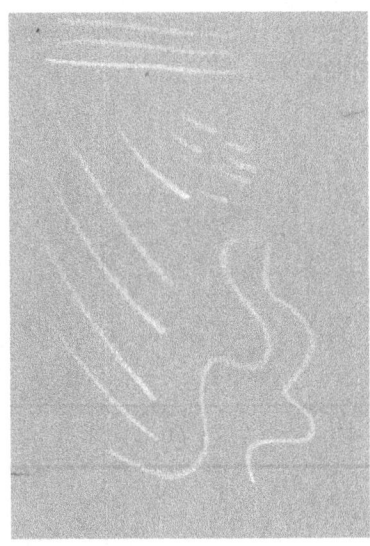

Fig. 6a. HB and 2B charcoal pencil   Fig. 6b. white charcoal pencil

6. Create gradations with blending

To create a gradation with blending, we first of all create the gradation with our willow charcoal either held on the side or with the large ellipse area on the chisel point tip (see Figs. 7a and 7b.) Once we have laid the charcoal down onto the page, we can then soften the area by blending with either a stump, cotton bud or both of these alternatively.

1. Break a short piece of thick willow charcoal and prepare it ready for large areas.
2. Create a gradation with this piece of charcoal by dragging it across the surface of the smooth side of your paper. This is the same technique your learned first of all in '**1. Cover large areas with willow charcoal.**' Press hard to begin with then ease off the pressure until the final touch is so delicate you are barely skimming the surface of your paper (see Fig. 7a.)

3. Using a clean paper stump, gently begin blending in the lightest area and make your way up into the darkest area. Try not to blend very much in the dark areas as you will find that the charcoal easily lifts off. If it does lift off too much, simply reapply another layer of charcoal and then leave it alone. By blending in the light area first it helps you to achieve a very light blend (see Fig. 7b.) If you begin in the dark area first, you will drag the charcoal particles from the top down into the lighter area making it too dark and therefore limiting the gradation.

4. Using another clean paper stump travel upwards a second time and even a third if needed, however do not over-blend or you will damage the surface of your page.

Tip: You can also use a cotton bud for blending and decide yourself which you prefer to use and when. In the example here (see Fig. 7b) a stump was used first then the cotton bud afterwards.

Fig. 7a. Willow charcoal on the side dragged across the page using varying pressure

Fig. 7b. Willow charcoal blended with a stump then cotton bud afterwards

7. Create soft edges with blending

Within the shaded areas of the shapes that you are shading, you will discover some very soft blurred edges. Soft edges are ***edges without a hard outline.*** They transition softly over a very short space from a darker tone into a lighter tone or visa-versa but have no hard outline. In the photograph here (see Fig. 8a) you can see a soft edge in the area surrounding the tip of the nose and nostril area. In the drawing alongside (see Fig. 8b) you can see the soft edge drawn with charcoal. The transition of tones in this area is so rapid that it still forms an edge around the shadow but the edge is softly blurred. You can create a soft edge with this process;

There is a soft edge surrounding the shape of this shadow around the tip of the nose and along the edge of the nostril area.

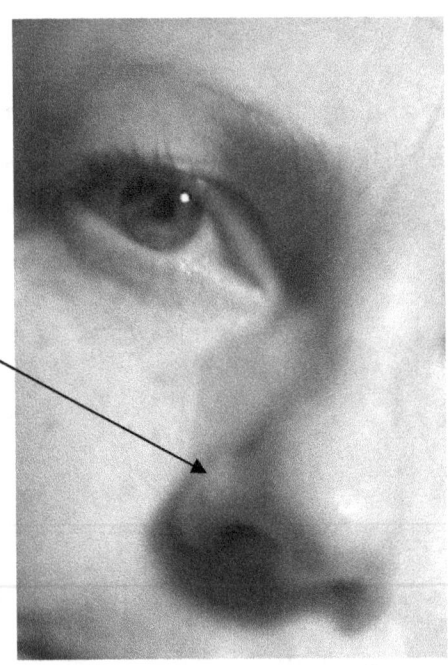

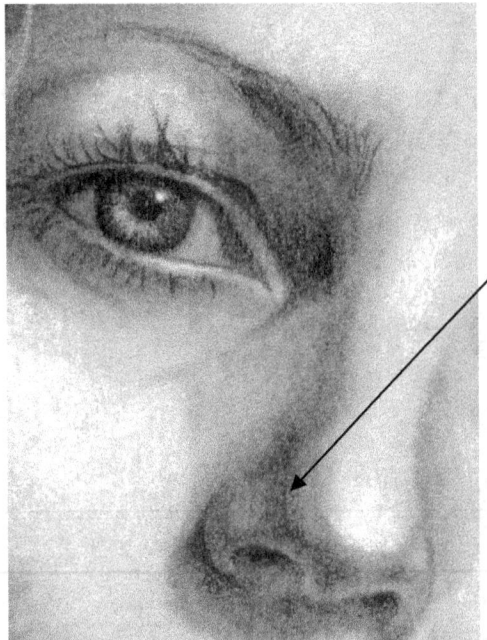

The soft edge rendered in charcoal.

Fig. 8a. Photograph of a soft edge   Fig. 8b. Charcoal drawing of a soft edge

1. Shade a small area using a short piece of your large willow charcoal stick held on the side and dragged across your page. Once you have laid on the charcoal, blend the area with a stump (see Fig. 8c.)

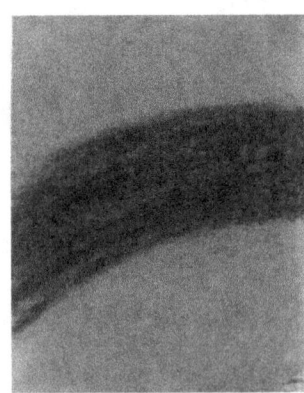

Fig. 8c.   Fig. 8d.

www.DrawPJ.com

2. Once blended with the stump, you can then draw the shape of the shadow with more willow charcoal (Fig. 8d.)

3. Once you have drawn the shape of your shadow on, you then have two options; if it is a really dark shadow you can just blend around the edges of the shape and leave the centre area of charcoal untouched (see Fig. 8e.)

4. If it is a medium-toned area you can blend the entire area as well as the edges, in that case you would blend the edges first and make your way towards the centre (see Fig. 8f.)

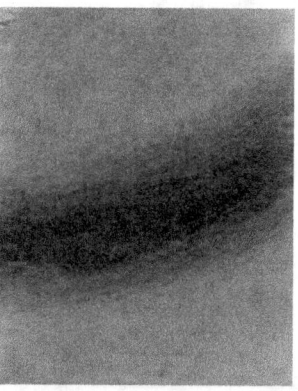

Fig. 8e.   Fig. 8f.

5. To create soft-edges in a lightly toned area, you can simply use your cotton bud dipped into the willow charcoal powder. Create the shaded area first, then simply blend out from that area afterwards (see Figs. 8g and 8h.)

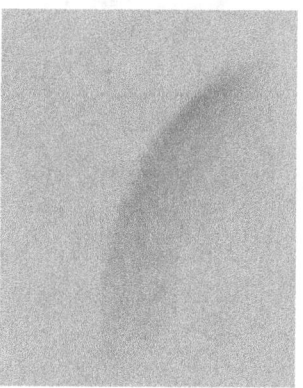   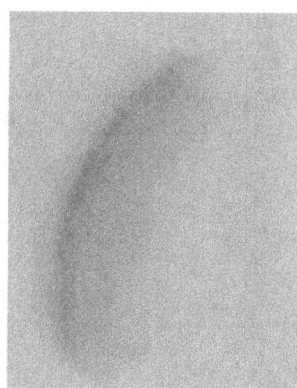

Fig. 8g.   Fig. 8h.

8. Create hard edges

Within the shaded areas of the object that you are drawing, you will also discover some hard, clean edges. Hard edges are areas of tones that transition instantly from a darker tone into a lighter tone or visa-versa. You can see a hard edge in the cheek area of this photograph here (see Fig. 9a.) The hard edge in the charcoal drawing has been created by the willow charcoal laid directly onto the grey paper (see Fig. 9b.)

There is a hard edge around the shape of this shadow on the cheek area.

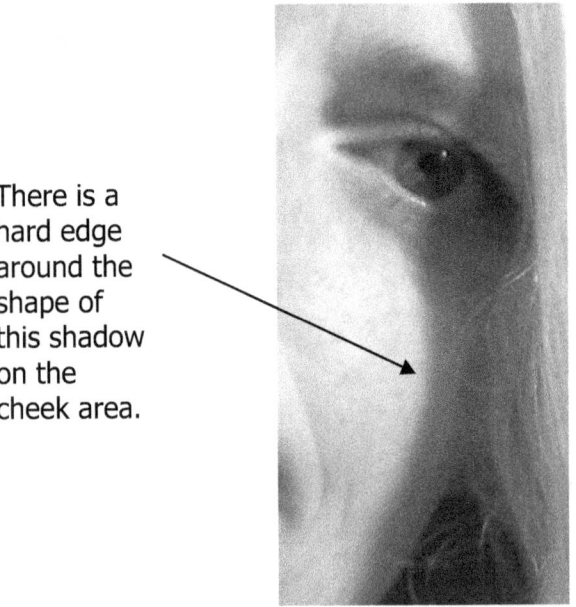

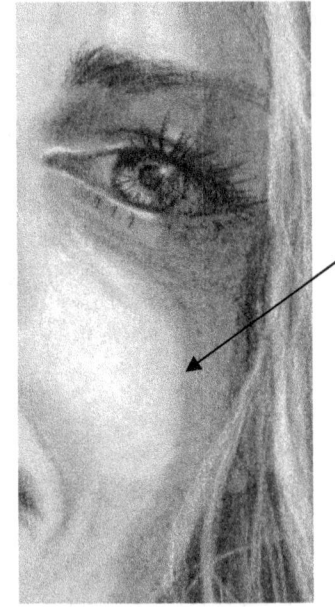

The hard edge rendered in charcoal.

Fig. 9a. Photograph of a hard edge   Fig. 9b. Charcoal drawing of a hard edge

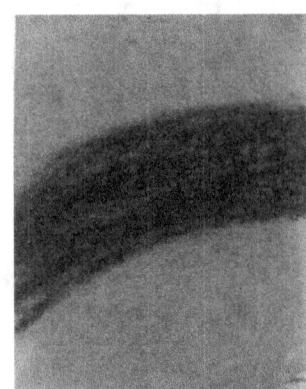

Fig. 9c.   Fig. 9d.

1. Shade a small area using a short piece of your large willow charcoal stick held on the side and dragged across your page. Once you have laid on the charcoal, blend the area with a stump (see Fig. 9c.)
2. Create a hard edge by drawing over the blended area with your willow charcoal stick. Begin by drawing the edge of the shape or line with the tip prepared with a chisel point. Once you have drawn the edge or outline of a shape, fill in the entire area right up to the edges using the ellipse shape of the chisel point (see Fig. 9d.) Your hard edge is already created. You can choose to either blend the area or not depending on how dark you wish to make it.

> **Tip:** The key to keeping a hard edge is to avoid blending the sides of the shape into the surrounding areas. You can 'tidy up' the edge by running your cotton bud along the sides of the area if needed but be careful not to disturb the line too much or you will create a soft edge.

3. You can also create another hard edge area by simply drawing a shape directly onto the grey paper (without shading the background first.) Draw a line first then shade outwards from the line with the wide ellipse shaped area on your thick willow charcoal stick. You can either blend this area or leave it as it is. In this picture the charcoal has been left untouched (see Fig. 9e.) The actual line along this hard-edge can vary in width for extra interest.
4. Create a very light hard edge area by simply using your cotton bud dipped into willow charcoal powder (see Fig. 9f.) Create the shape first then shade backwards from that line. This is a useful technique in the delicate areas of a face in portraiture such as the cheek and mouth areas.

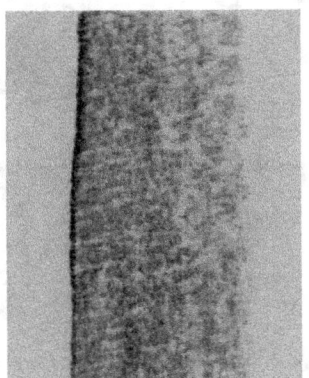
Fig. 9e.

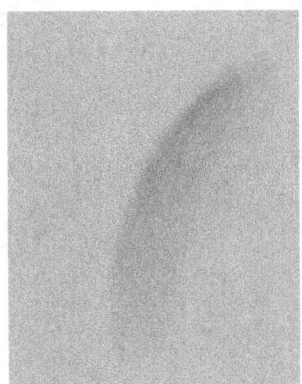
Fig. 9f.

9. Hatching lines with willow charcoal and charcoal pencil

You can create hatching lines with either your charcoal pencil (see Fig. 10a) or thin willow charcoal stick prepared with a chisel point (see Fig. 10c.) You can blend the willow charcoal hatching lines (see Fig. 10d.) You can also combine both willow charcoal hatching (blended) and the charcoal pencil together (see Fig. 10e.)

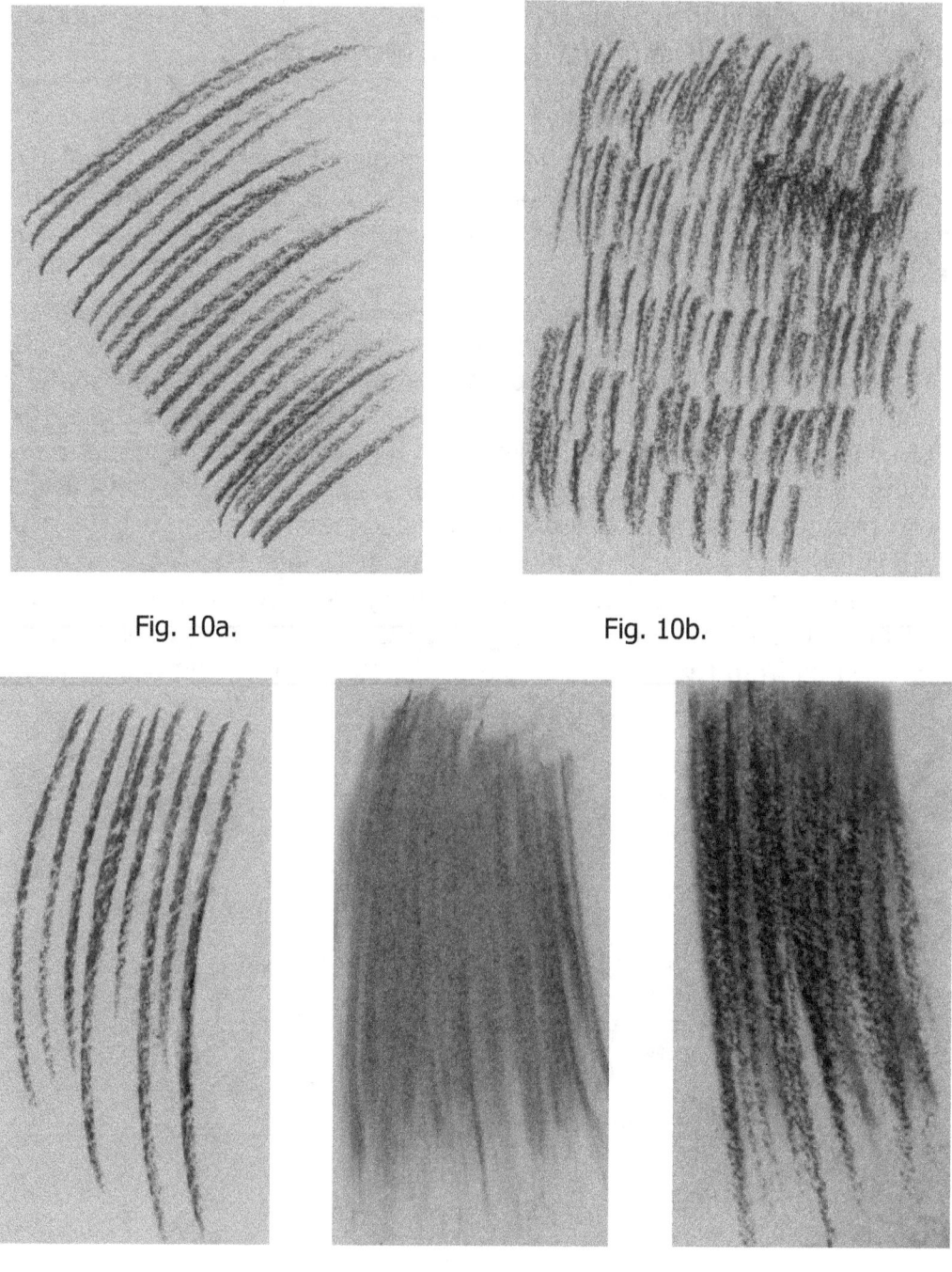

Fig. 10a.   Fig. 10b.

Fig. 10c.   Fig. 10d.   Fig. 10e

1. Create an area of hatching using your **_charcoal pencil_** sharpened to a point (see Fig. 10a.) Place the pencil on the page and use a flicking motion as you drag your pencil upwards releasing the pressure as you travel. Work quickly and try hard to keep the lines parallel to one another. If you use the flicking motion, your lines will naturally taper making them thinner and paler in tone on the ends. This stroke is helpful when drawing hair. Try drawing long strokes and also some short hatching strokes (see Fig. 10b.) Remember to keep your elbow out to the side, this encourages you to use your full arm motion.

2. Create an area of hatching using your thin **_willow charcoal stick_** prepared with the chisel point (see Fig. 10c.) You will find that you don't have as much control when using the willow stick versus the charcoal pencil, however the willow stick is more easily blended. There isn't much taper either with the willow stick.

3. Blend the area using your stump by stroking the charcoal in the same direction as you applied the hatching stroke (see Fig. 10d.) This will soften and blur the area but retain the texture of the strokes.

4. Finally apply some charcoal pencil hatching lines over the top (see Fig. 10e.) This is a great texture for hair, fur, grass etc.

10. Lines with variations in width

Often when we are drawing we need to use lines with varying widths (see Figs. 11a and 11b.) There are times for example; when you will need to draw a very narrow line which then changes to a wider line and back to narrow one again. These changes in line widths often need to be gradual transitions but not always. They can also be sudden changes from wide to narrow or vice versa. You can use either your charcoal pencil, or willow charcoal stick prepared with the chisel point tip. With both of these tools, the same technique is used.

1. Prepare your **_thin willow stick_** with the chisel point tip as shown earlier in these notes. You will need to continually prepare this tip and may find your willow stick wears down very quickly needing to be replaced.

2. Create fine lines and curves with varying thicknesses using your thin willow charcoal stick (see Fig. 11a.) To do this, hold the stick on the tip touching your page (almost vertical to the page.) To create wider areas in the line, apply slightly more pressure and simply rub your willow charcoal stick back and forth to form the shape of the line as you do so. Don't press too hard or the tip will shatter.

3. Create lines and curves with varying thickness using the same technique with your **_charcoal pencil_** (see Fig. 11b.)

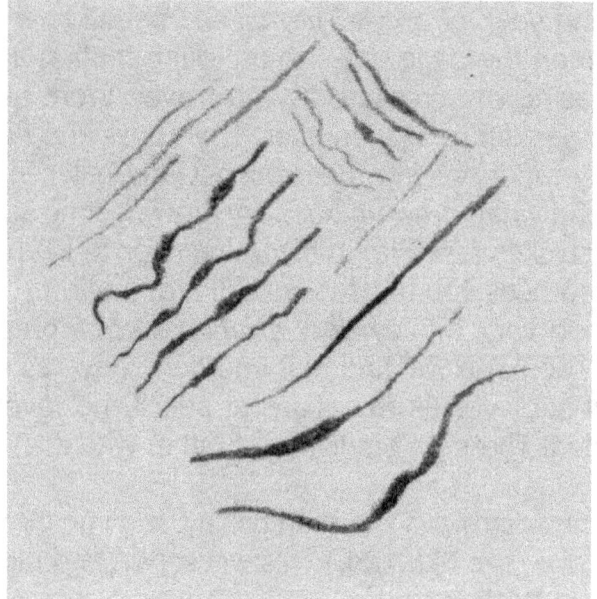
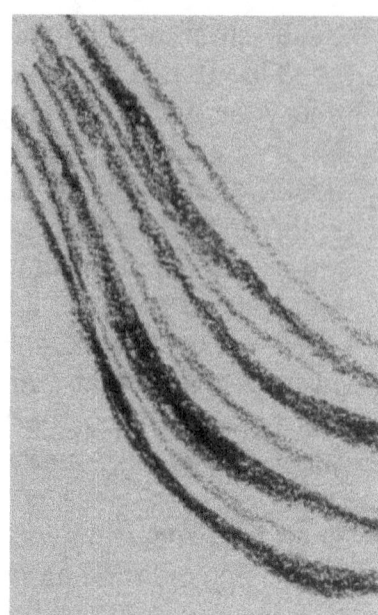

Fig. 11a.   Fig. 11b.

4. There are many different ways you can draw these varying widths in lines. Try drawing some curved lines with your willow charcoal, and then shade the areas underneath the curves with the larger ellipse shaped area of the chisel point (see Fig. 11c.)

5. Blend the area beneath the line using your stump (see Fig 11d.)

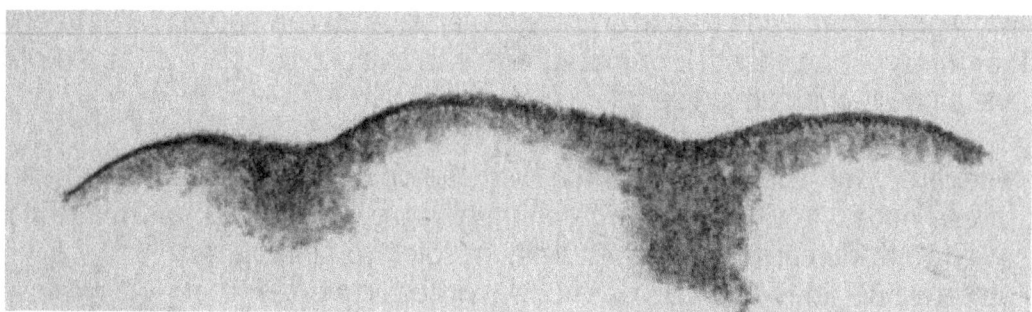

Fig. 11c.

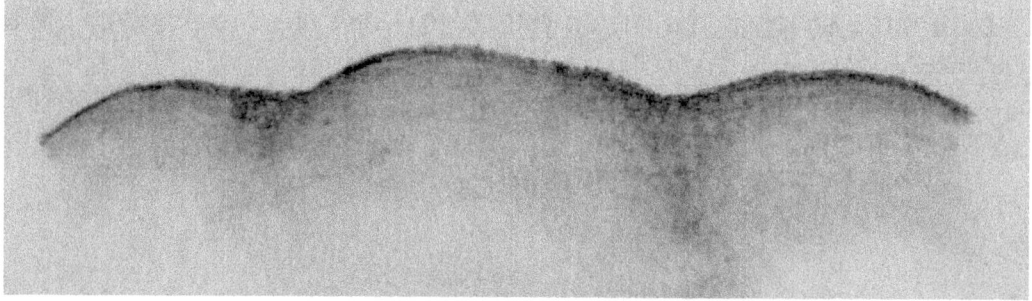

Fig. 11d.

11. Experiment with erasing techniques

Within your list of supplies you were asked to purchase three different types of erasers; a gum eraser, putty eraser and a hard plastic (or click eraser.) In this section we will look at the various uses of each different eraser. It is important to understand that the eraser is not simply used for removing mistakes. The eraser when used with charcoal is also a drawing tool. You can draw into any area that has been covered by charcoal, using your erasers. Each eraser will achieve a different effect and therefore suit a slightly different purpose.

1. Before you begin, please shade the entire square that was set aside for this technique on your sheet of Mi-Teintes paper. Use a thick piece of willow charcoal dragged across the surface, then blend the area afterwards with your paper stump.
2. Divide the square into 4 sections using your charcoal pencil on top of the shaded area of charcoal by halving it horizontally and vertically (see Fig. 12a.) You will be creating four different eraser techniques; one in each of these four quarters.

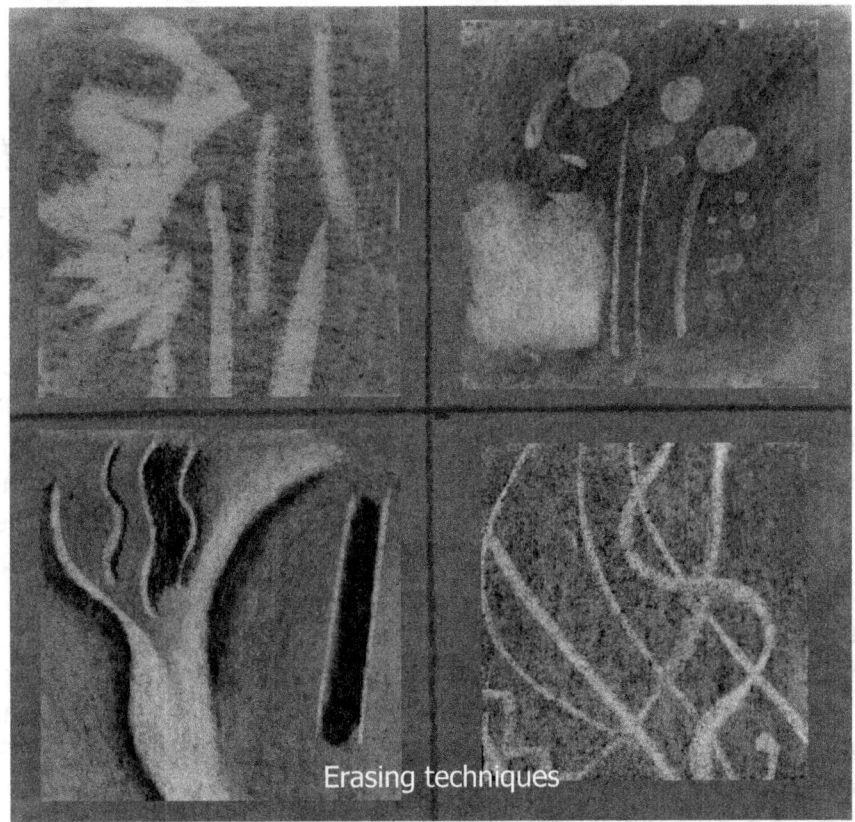

Fig. 12a. Example of the shaded square with 4 different erasing techniques

3. In the top left quarter of the square, draw some lines and marks into the layer of charcoal with your gum eraser (see Fig. 12b.) Notice the kinds of marks it makes as you remove the charcoal. The gum eraser is great for erasing larger areas and thick lines. It is very crumbly so that you cannot easily ruin your paper, making it ideal for erasing more stubborn charcoal marks. It is also quite large and cumbersome so it isn't suitable for finer details.

   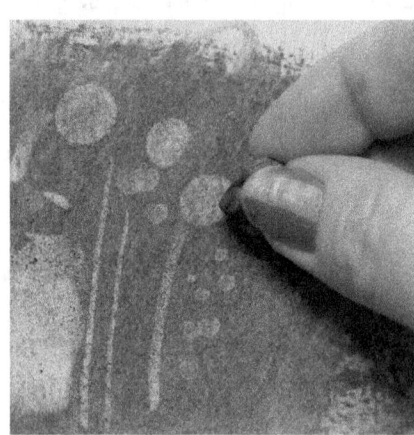

Fig. 12b.   Fig. 12c.

4. In the top right quarter of the larger square remove some areas with your putty eraser to see the kinds of marks you can make. You can draw very fine lines and larger shapes with the putty eraser (see Fig. 12c.) Working with just a small piece, you can mould the putty eraser into different shapes depending on your needs. Try preparing it so that it becomes a small ball with a point on the end like an ice-cream cone (see Fig. 12c.) or you can squash it as flat as a sheet of thin cardboard. Whatever way you prepare your putty eraser just be aware that you will need to continually re-mould it as it fills with charcoal very quickly. After several swipes across the area it will need re-shaping.

5. In the bottom left quarter of your large shaded square, try a combination of putty eraser and lines and curves added to the outside of the erased shapes with your willow charcoal or charcoal pencil. Blend some of these charcoal areas (see Fig. 12d.)

6. In the bottom right quarter draw some lines and curves (see Fig. 12f) using your hard plastic or click eraser. You can cut the tip on an angle either on one side or both sides to form a chisel or 'V' shape tip. This eraser has been cut with a craft knife into a 'V' shaped tip (see Fig. 12e insert. The 'V' shape is outlined in purple.) The click eraser is fantastic because it feels like you are using a pencil and is especially helpful when drawing single strands of hair to finish off your portrait with. You can achieve very fine lines by continually sharpening your click eraser this way.

Putty-erased area. ——————

Charcoal pencil added to form a hard line. ——————

Charcoal pencil added then blended in with a stump.

Willow charcoal is added then blended, forming a hard edge between the line and the erased area.

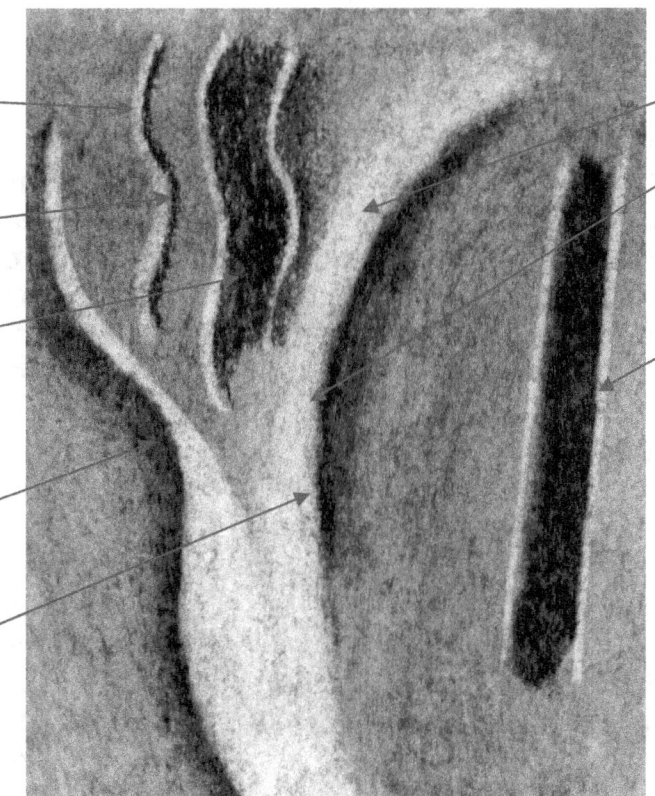

Putty-erased area.

Putty eraser was used in this area.

Fig. 12d.

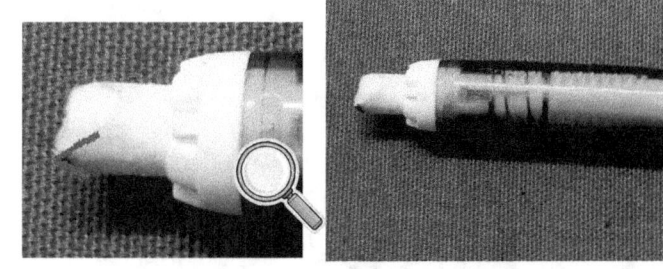

Fig. 12e. A click eraser with chisel point

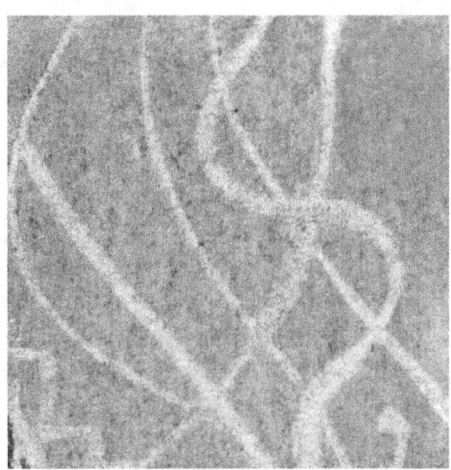

Fig. 12f.

12. White conte and white charcoal techniques

White Conté is a type of Crayon with a square cross-section which is especially designed to make it easier to break. Conté has been used by many of the great masters of art including Degas and Picasso to name a few. It is most found in; white, black and sepia. These crayons are made from a mixture of clay and graphite and are waxier and firmer than soft pastel. They work well with willow charcoal and the bright white colour provides a perfect highlight when working on coloured paper. When working on light grey paper (as we are here) the white Conté becomes our level 1 value in relation to a value scale and the grey paper is the level 2 value.

1. Break your white Conté stick into halves and then sharpen the tip to form a chisel point by rubbing across your rough sandpaper; just as you did with the willow charcoal earlier in these course notes.
2. You can experiment by either using the tip of the Conté or laying it on the side and dragging it across the surface of your page to cover larger areas. Vary the pressure as you rub your Conté into the page so that you can notice the difference between areas with varying pressure applied.
3. A white charcoal pencil is great for hatching and long thin lines as well as small details due to its ease of handling and very fine tip when sharpened correctly. Be careful not to sharpen this one with a blunt sharpener or it will crumble easily. Try your hand at some hatching strokes and wavy lines with the white charcoal pencil as well (see Fig. 13.b.)

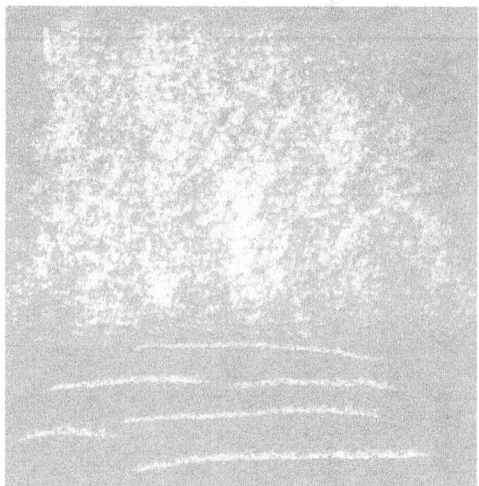 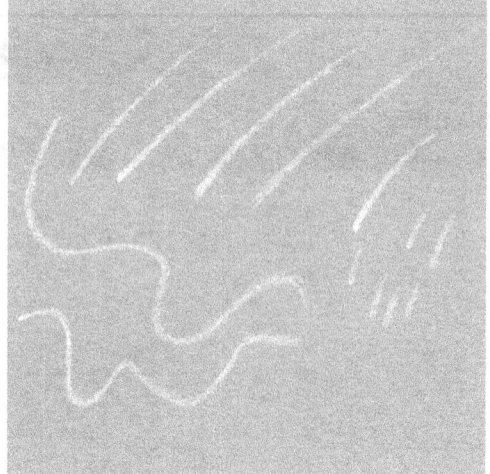

Fig. 13a   Fig. 13b

Tip: With portraiture we can use white Conté just softly to form a sparkle on the skin in the areas that protrude forward into the light such as the forehead, beneath and above the eyebrow areas, cheek-bone, nose, lips and chin (see Figs. 14a and 14b.) Charcoal pencil is good for highlights in the strands of hair and white Conté in larger sections of highlight.

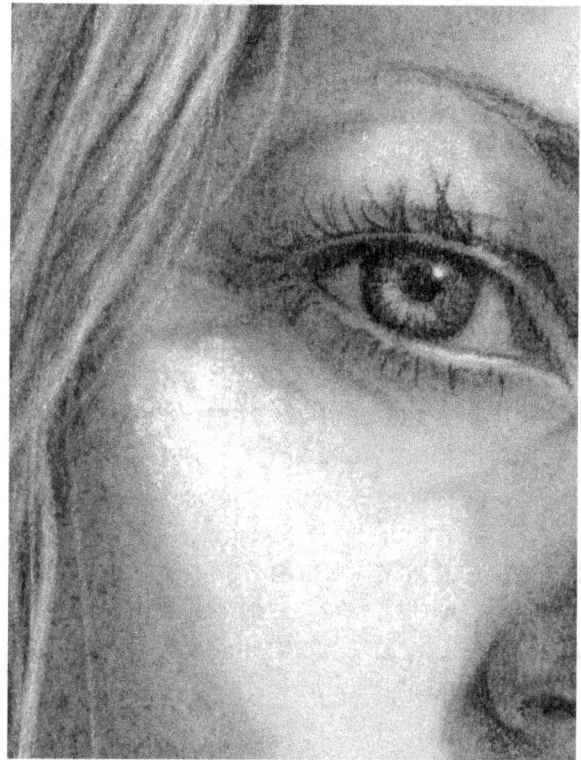

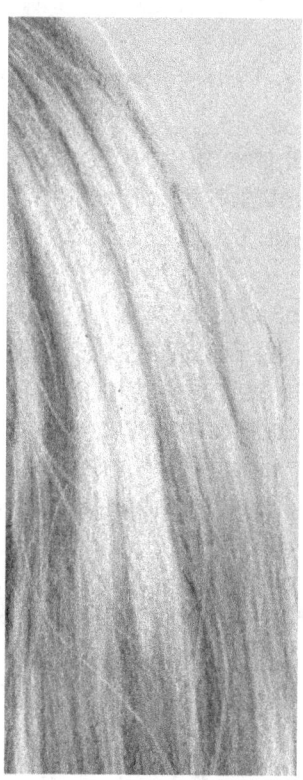

Fig. 14a   Fig. 14b

Summary for week one

To truly master charcoal as an art medium is one of the most wonderful and rewarding things you will ever achieve as an artist. To be able to create images using just a humble stick of burnt wood is an incredible feeling. From the tiniest most delicate markings to the broadest and darkest strokes, charcoal is a truly versatile and magnificent medium.

Once we begin to understand exactly how intuitive charcoal is, we discover that the more we smile and relax, the better our results will be. Saying encouraging things to yourself will really help you achieve better results. Smile to relax your entire upper torso and love your work into creation. 'Just show up at your table' and the rest will take care of itself! Often the hardest part is just sitting there in front of your work and to begin. Have a fun week and enjoy the journey.

Week Two

Introduction to week two

During this second week of your course, you be shown how to draw three different and popular hairstyles. The techniques you learn here can be adapted to a huge variety of other hairstyles and so many other subjects too, including animal fur among many things. You are only limited by your imagination with these techniques.

General information on drawing hair

One of the most important things to consider when you are drawing realistic hair is to concentrate on depicting the overall structure first. Look with your eyes squinted to help you see the outline and then the major light and dark masses within the outline.

The masses include the shapes that are formed by the root areas on the top of the scalp, the outlines that the hair forms around the cheek, temple and forehead areas as well as the outline around the outside of the hair itself. Drawing the overall shape of the major masses will help your drawings of hair appear more realistic rather than attempting to draw individual hairs. The individual hairs are also important, however, they should not to be over-emphasised.

It is the contrast of the occasional strands of hair drawn in against the broader areas of tonal contrast that create interest and the overall impression of hair. The placement of several carefully placed hairs can successfully depict realistic hair far more easily and effectively than if you draw in many individual hairs.

Exercise for week two: choose your first hairstyle to draw

Begin this exercise by selecting from one of the three exercises provided in the small samples. In the samples on the following pages, you will see a photograph of the hairstyle then alongside the photograph you will see the charcoal rendering of that hairstyle (see Fig. 15a, 15b, 15c, 15d, 15e and 15f.)

The methods taught in all three of these hairstyles are adaptable to many others. Once you have made your selection, proceed to the appropriate section for the chosen hairstyle titled '**Step-by-step Instructions for....**'

 It is highly recommended that you complete all three hairstyles to gain a good solid understanding of how to draw hair.

1. Adult Female Long Hair (see Figs. 15a and 15b)

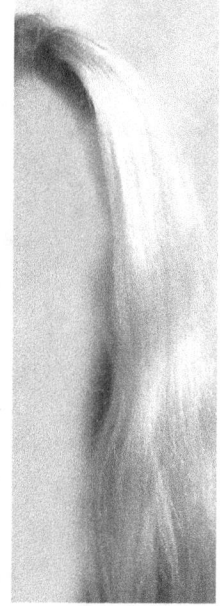

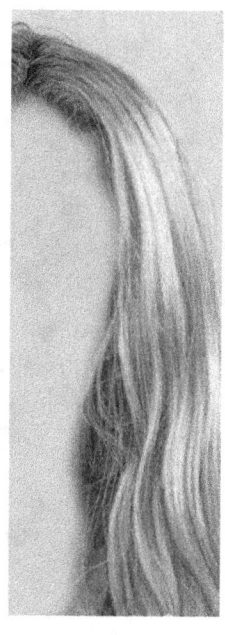

Fig. 15a   Fig. 15b

2. Adult Male Short Hair (see Figs. 15c and 15d)

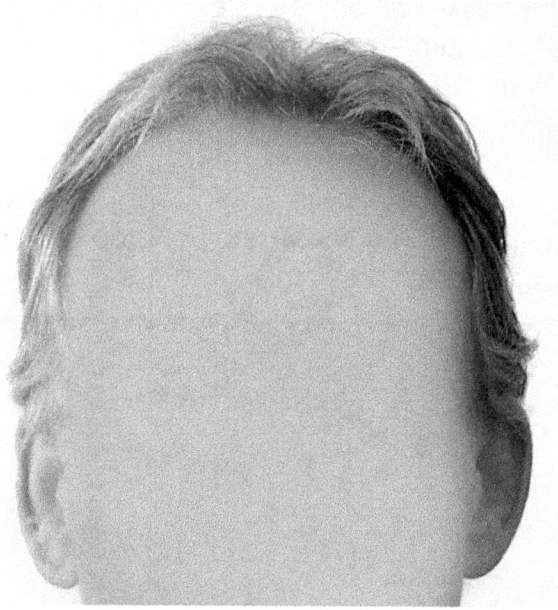

Fig. 15c   Fig. 15d

3. Adult Female Curly Hair (see Figs. 15e and 15f)

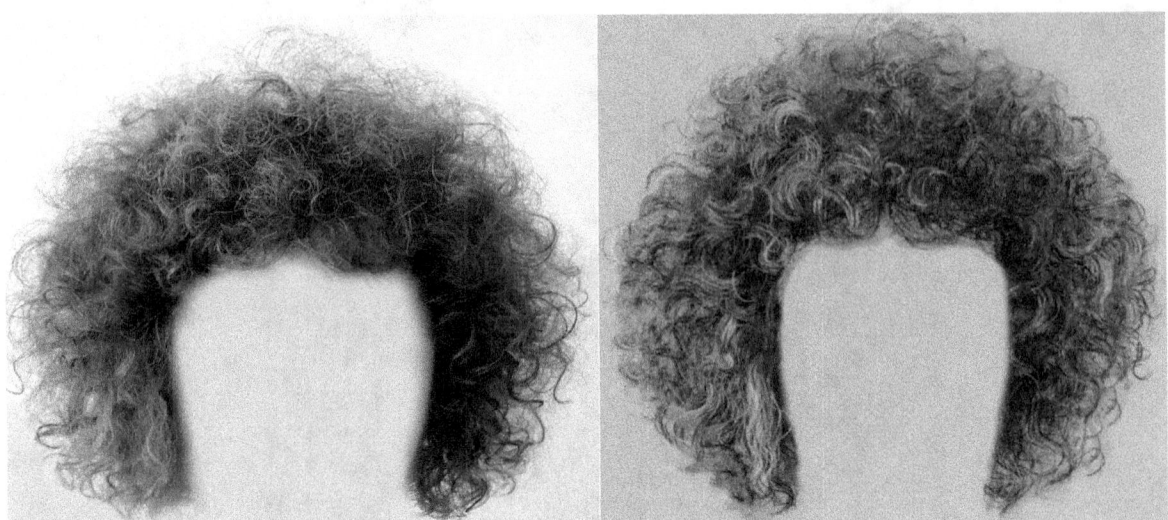

Fig. 15e   Fig. 15f

Tip: For all three hairstyles, please work with a six-tone value scale. This means six different tones from light to dark, beginning with number one as the white conte and number 2 as the tone of the grey paper. Numbers 3, 4, 5 and 6 should gradually become darker and darker by using pressure and more charcoal as you travel higher in number.

Draw this value scale as a series of small squares all in a line at the very top of your page and refer to this often during the creation of your drawing.

Step-by-step Instructions for hairstyle one: Adult Female Long Hair

In this hairstyle example you will be drawing just a section of long hair within a rectangular box as shown in the photograph and drawing here (see Figs 16a. and 16b.) Please use the photograph as your main reference source (print it out on high quality photo paper if you like) and the drawings as an example of the step-by-step process. Work expressively and use your whole arm to draw. Make sure that you draw on the smooth side of a sheet of grey Mi-Teintes paper.

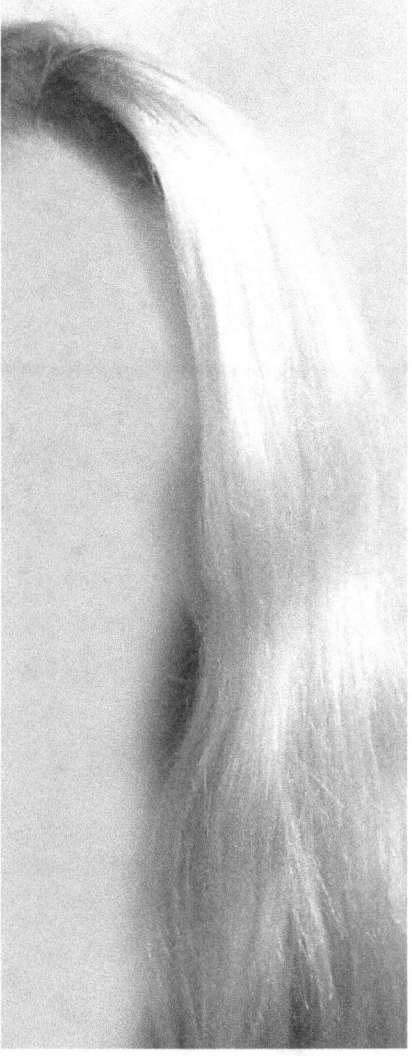

Fig. 16a Photograph

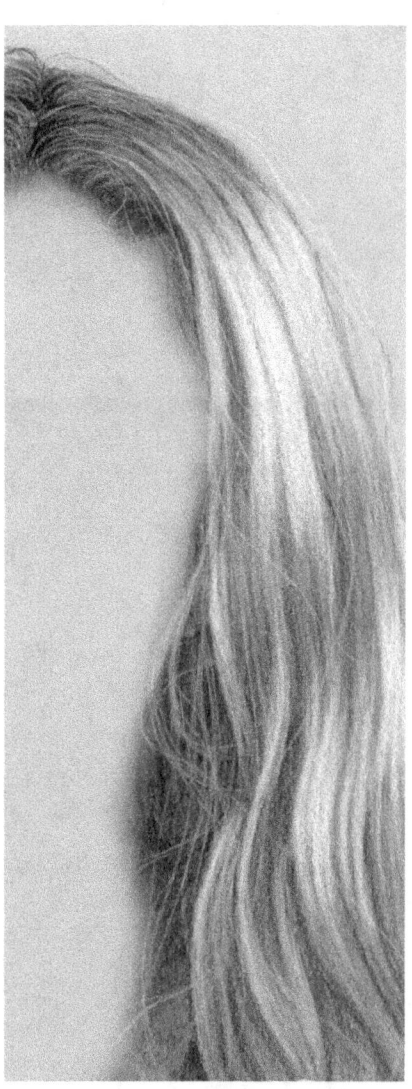

Fig. 16b Charcoal drawing

Step One: Draw the outline of the hair

1. Use your HB charcoal pencil to draw a rectangular box measuring 5.5cm wide by 14cm high (see Fig. 17a.) You will be drawing the section of long hair inside this box.
2. Measure and mark half way dashes on all four sides of your rectangle (see Fig. 16a.) Please note: the rectangle here may not be the same size depending on your printer settings.
3. Draw the initial outline of the hair (see Fig. 16b) by comparing the angles and curves to the half-way marks. Use the very tip of your *willow charcoal stick* shaped to a chisel point.

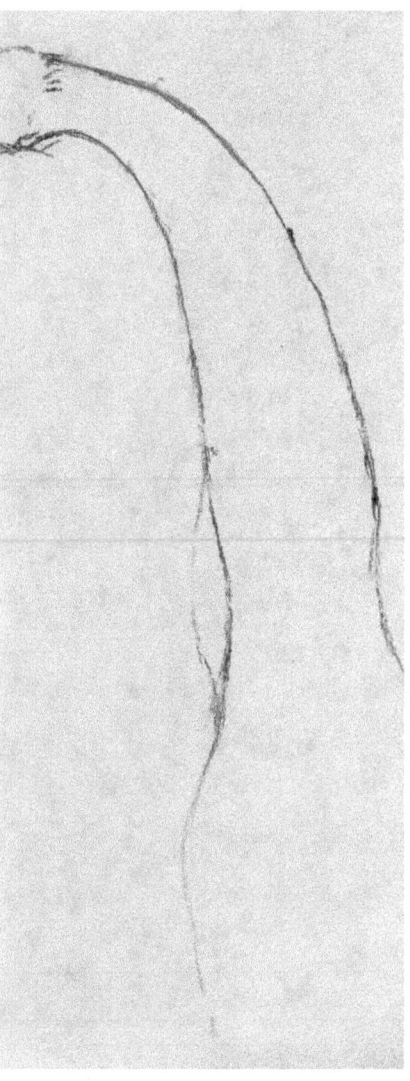

Fig. 17a   Fig. 17b.

Tip: Resist the temptation to draw all of your early markings with your charcoal pencil as it is difficult to erase. Use your willow charcoal as it is much easier to erase than your charcoal pencil.

Step Two: Begin to shade the roots of the hair

In this step we will begin to shade in the darker mass of the root area and introduce the general direction of the hair. Always refer to the photograph as your main reference and the drawings as an example. Use self-expression and not an exact copy line for line. This should be an enjoyable process. Allow your whole body to become involved by drawing from your shoulder rather than just your wrist. Draw expressively and with confidence. You can easily erase if you are not pleased with your markings.

1. Use a stick of willow charcoal with some hatching lines to shade the roots of the hair then blend these with a stump following the direction of the lines (see Fig. 18a.)
2. Add some more hatching lines with your 2B charcoal pencil always being aware of the major direction of your lines (see Fig. 18b.) Think about the hair and where it comes from. The outside layers of long hair drop directly from the roots on top of the scalp.

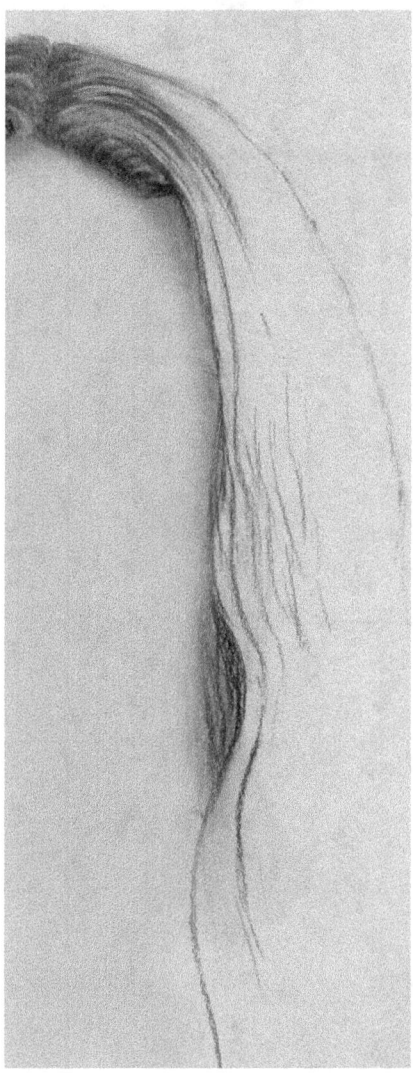
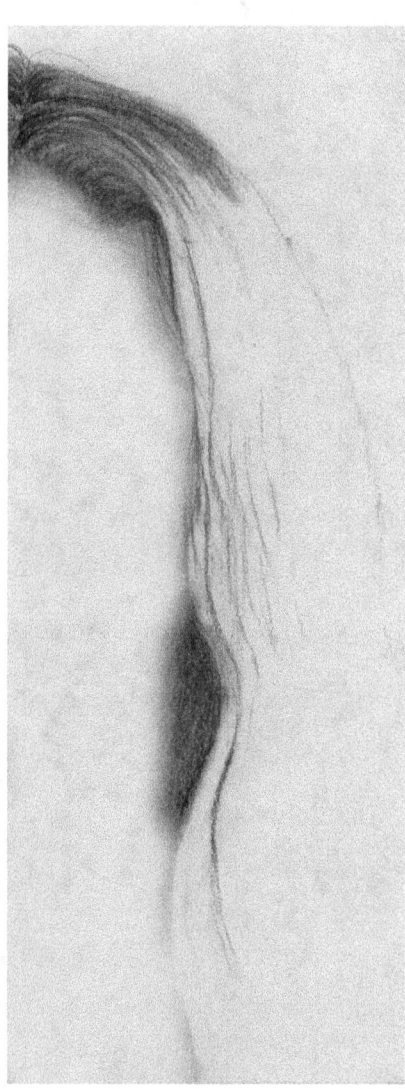

Fig. 18a   Fig. 18b.

Step Three: Begin to shade the major dark areas

1. Prepare a short piece of thick charcoal with a chisel point.
2. Use the large ellipse-shaped area to shade in the dark shadow areas of the hair. Press lightly as these will only become a level 4 tone. You will see these more easily by squinting. Follow the general direction of the hair.
3. Draw some curved lines in with the tip of the willow charcoal in the narrower shaded areas to help define the individual clumps of hair (see Fig. 19a.)
4. Add some fine wispy hairs to the top of the hair and around the forehead with your 2B charcoal pencil sharpened to a very fine point.
5. Draw fine strands of light hair into the darker areas with your click eraser.
6. Blend these areas with your paper stump following the direction of the hair (see Fig. 19b.) Always think about the hair and which direction it is flowing in when you are drawing lines, shading or blending.

Add some fine wispy hairs with your 2B charcoal pencil.

Draw some curved lines with the tip of the willow charcoal stick to help define the major clumps of hair.

Use your click eraser to draw some light hairs into the dark areas.

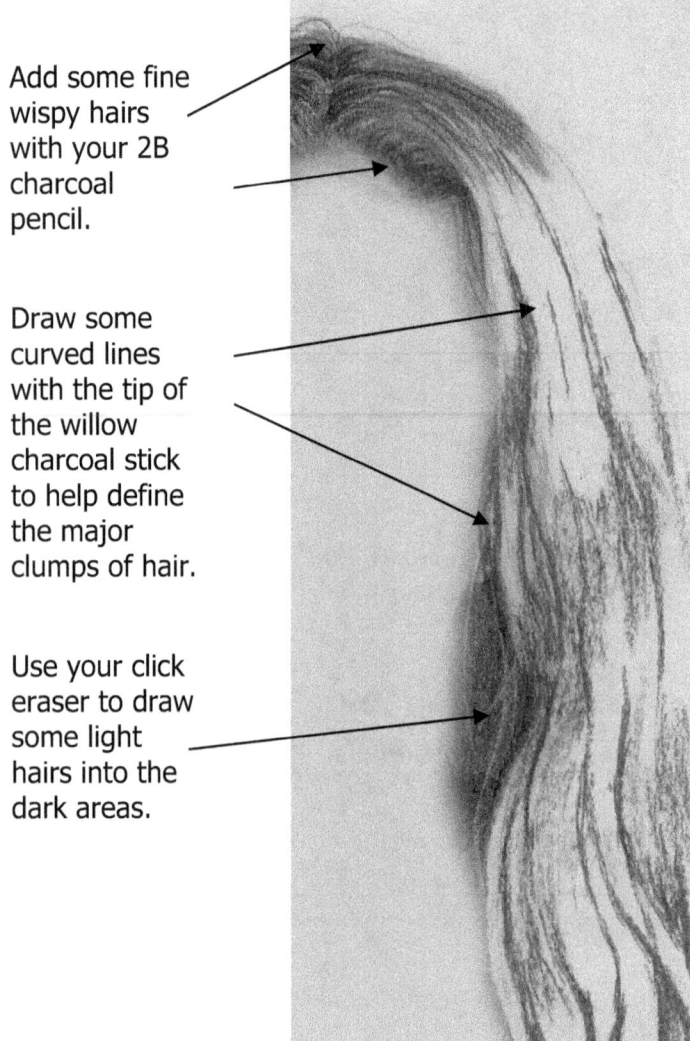

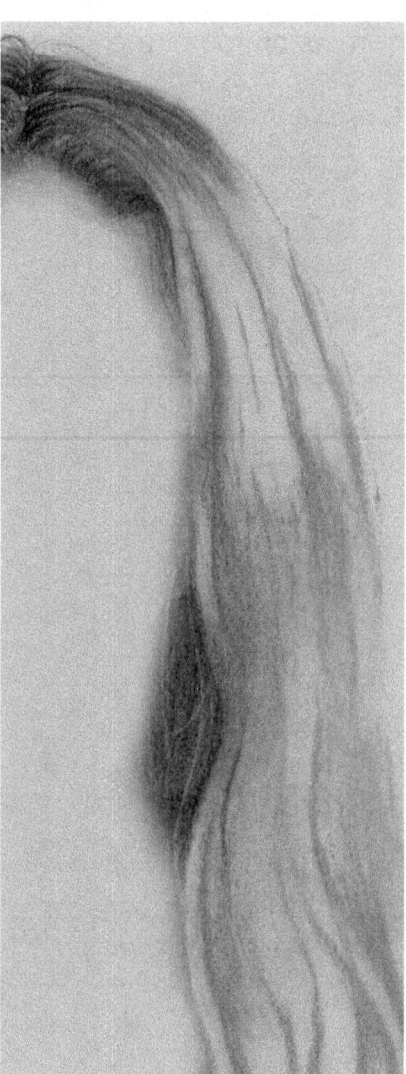

Fig. 19a

Fig. 19b.

www.DrawPJ.com

Step Four: Refine the texture of the hair

1. Go back over the darker areas using your 2B charcoal pencil and create fine lines and curves using the hatching stroke. Hatch first in one direction then in the other within each dark mass, carefully overlapping the strokes in the centre of the mass. The finer tapering ends of the hatching strokes will provide a gradual transition into the highlighted areas (see insert 20.)
2. Outline some of the clumps of the hair with your 2B charcoal pencil and add some very fine wispy hairs with a HB charcoal pencil.

This is the effect we are aiming to achieve with the hatching.

This is how you draw the hatching lines so that the base areas are hidden within the area and taper outwards towards the edges.

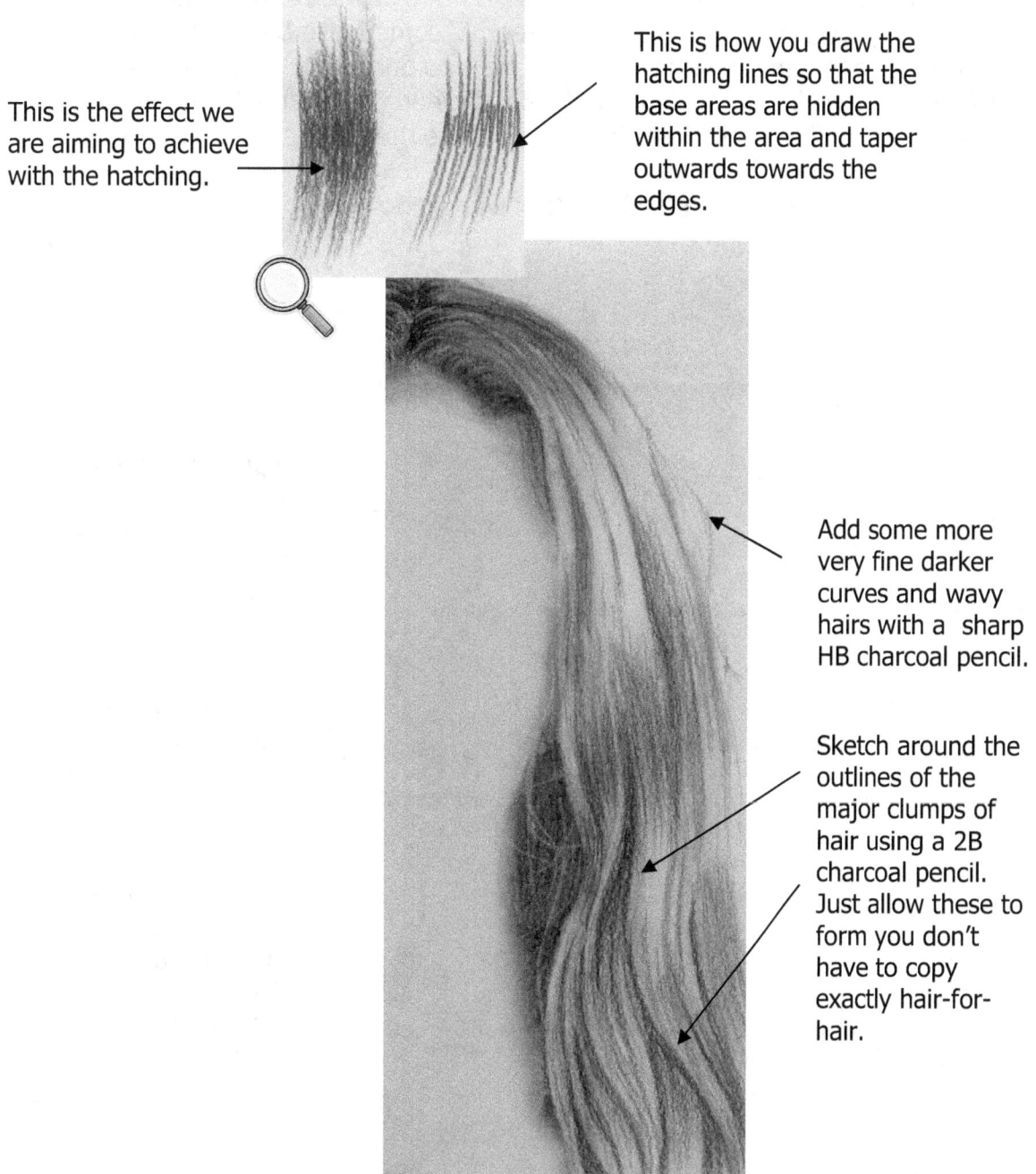

Add some more very fine darker curves and wavy hairs with a sharp HB charcoal pencil.

Sketch around the outlines of the major clumps of hair using a 2B charcoal pencil. Just allow these to form you don't have to copy exactly hair-for-hair.

Fig. 20

© 2023 Cindy Wider. All Rights Reserved.
The contents of this course may not be used, sold, reproduced or distributed without written permission from Cindy Wider.

Final Step: Add the white Conte and white charcoal

1. Use your white Conté stick prepared to a chisel point and hatch some curved lines into the lightest highlights. Work in the middle areas of the larger sections that have been left as the grey paper (see Fig. 21.) Follow the direction of the hair and remember that you are still drawing hair even though these are the reflection areas (highlights).
2. Add finishing touches to highlighted areas using the tip of a sharpened white charcoal pencil. Use the same procedure with your hatching that you used with the darker 2B charcoal; hatch outwards from the centre of the lightest areas.
3. Add fine wispy curves and waves to 'free up' some loose bits of hair, creating movement and a more natural appearance. You don't have to over-do this, just a few strategically placed hairs will be sufficient. Think about the shape and position of the fine hairs briefly before you place them, but then let your instinct and self-expression take over.
4. You also must know when to stop. Your work is now complete.

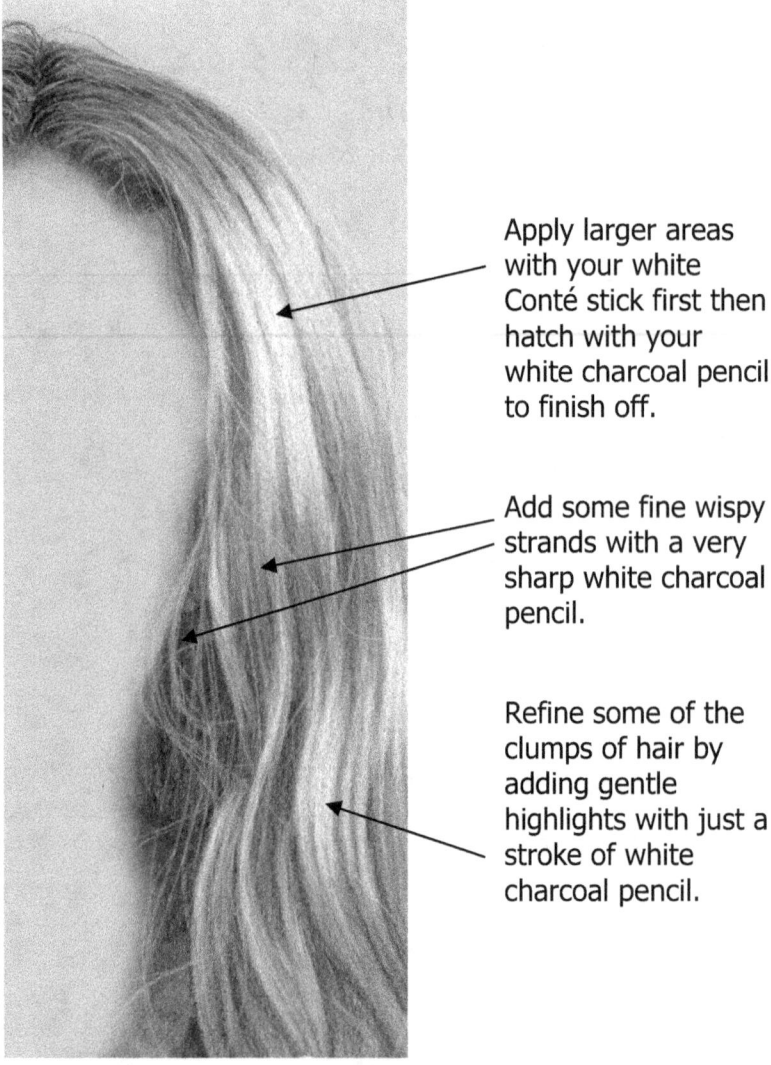

Apply larger areas with your white Conté stick first then hatch with your white charcoal pencil to finish off.

Add some fine wispy strands with a very sharp white charcoal pencil.

Refine some of the clumps of hair by adding gentle highlights with just a stroke of white charcoal pencil.

Fig. 21

www.DrawPJ.com

Create a template for the head shape

In this extra step you are shown how to accurately draw an egg-shape for the face using a template as a guide. Before you begin drawing either of the following two hairstyles (the adult male short hair or the adult female curly hair) you will need to draw a basic egg shape for the head. An easy way to draw the egg shape is to make a cardboard template for yourself. A green-coloured piece of cardboard was used here to create the template. You can use the cardboard from a cereal box or even a sheet of paper is fine. You only need to draw a half of the head then use this to flip over and copy the other half exactly.

1. Use your ruler to draw a vertical line down your page measuring 17cm using your HB charcoal pencil then make a small dash at the half-way mark.
2. Rule a horizontal line out from the half-way mark (making sure it is at a right angle to the vertical line) measuring 6cm long.
3. Sketch in the half egg-shape similar to the one you see here (see Fig. 22.) Note that this shape shown in Fig. 22 is not drawn to size.
4. Cut the half egg-shape out.
5. Use this as a template to draw around with your willow charcoal stick. Trace one half first then flip it over for the other half. Make sure you use the **smooth side of your Mi-Teintes paper** to draw on and allow plenty of room for some hair around the outside of the egg.

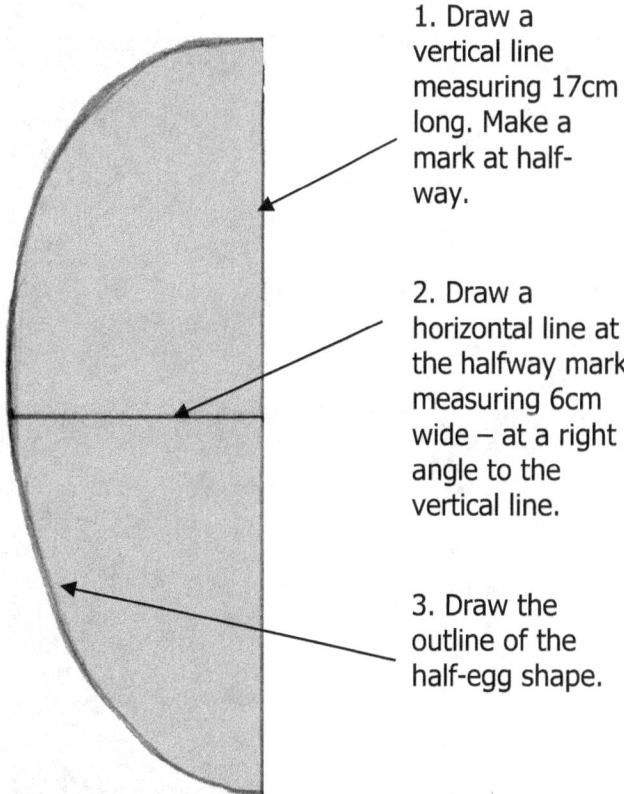

1. Draw a vertical line measuring 17cm long. Make a mark at half-way.

2. Draw a horizontal line at the halfway mark measuring 6cm wide – at a right angle to the vertical line.

3. Draw the outline of the half-egg shape.

Fig. 22. an example of a template for half of the head

Step-by-step Instructions for Hairstyle Two: Adult Male Short Hair

In this hairstyle example there is very little hair to draw with your willow charcoal and dark charcoal pencil. You will be drawing quite a lot with your white charcoal pencil. The hair will be drawn on the basic head template as mentioned above. Please use the photograph as your main reference source (see Fig. 23a) and the final drawing (see Fig. 23b) along with the other drawings as a guide for the step-by-step process. Work expressively and use your whole arm to draw. Refer to these drawings as often as needed. Make sure that you draw on the smooth side of a sheet of grey Mi-Teintes paper.

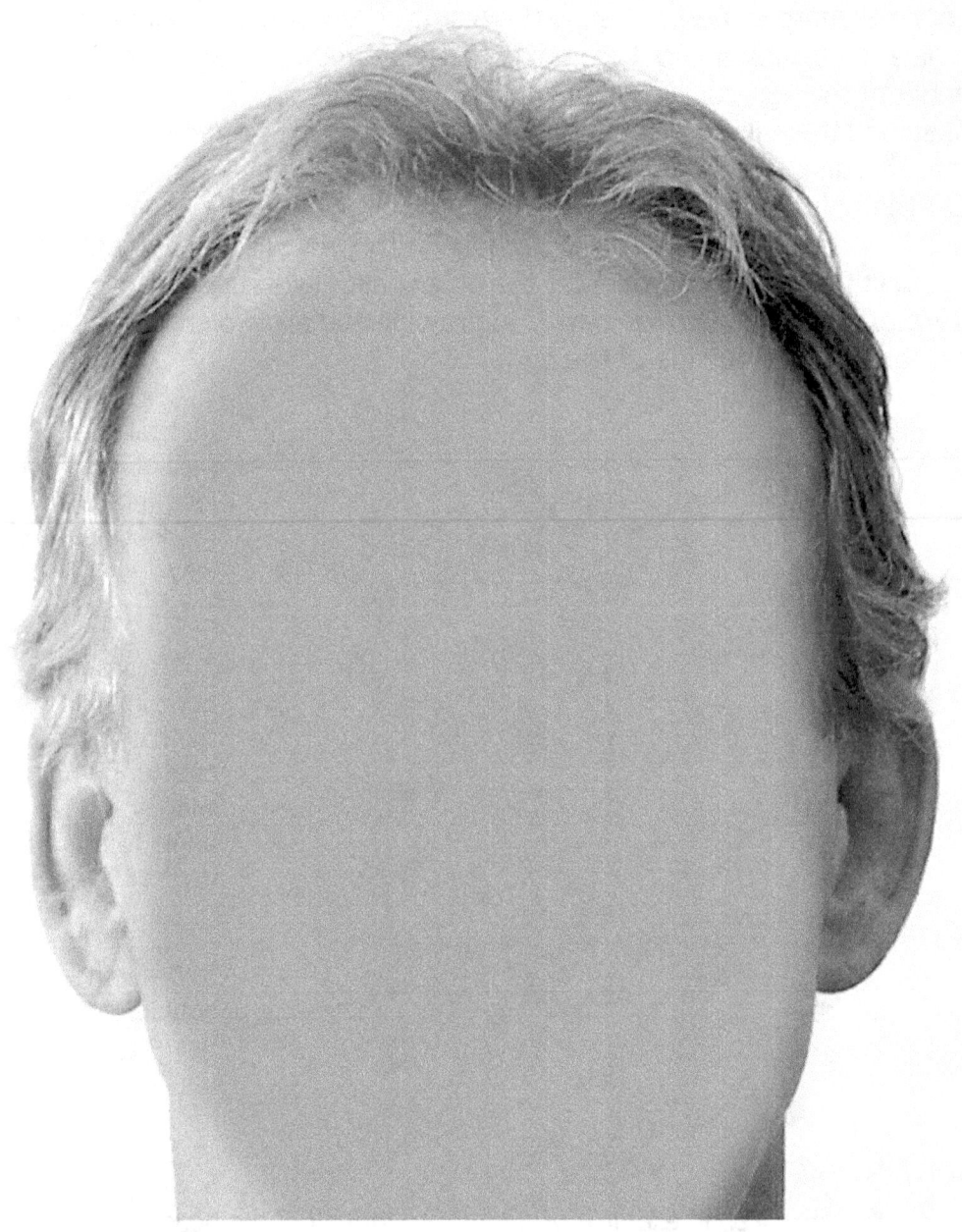

Fig. 23a. Photograph of adult male short hair

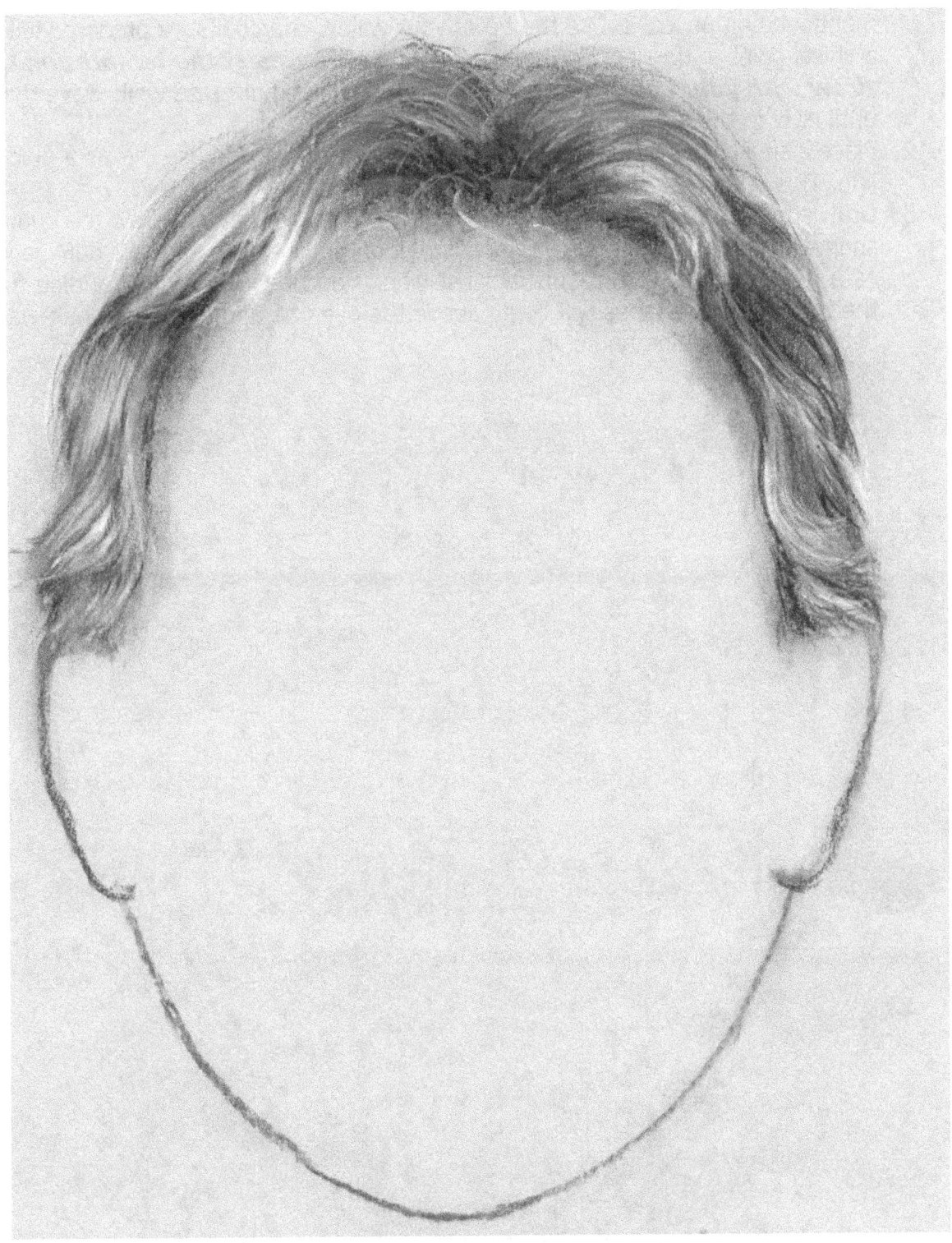

Fig. 23b. Charcoal drawing of adult male short hair

www.DrawPJ.com

Step One: Draw the head shape and position the ears

1. Begin by drawing the basic egg-shape for a head using your template as mentioned on page 33. Use the tip of your willow charcoal stick prepared with a chisel point to do all of your initial drawing with. ***Resist the temptation to draw with your charcoal pencil*** as it doesn't blend or erase well. Save that until later in the drawing.
2. Place a small mark in the very centre of the egg-shape and use this as a guide line. This is your eye-line.
3. Draw some curved shapes to indicate ears. You do not have to draw the entire shapes of the ears, just the basic construction outline. The ears are only used as a guide for you to measure against when you draw your initial outline for the hair. The ear shapes will begin above the eye-line and end about half-way between the eye-line and chin.

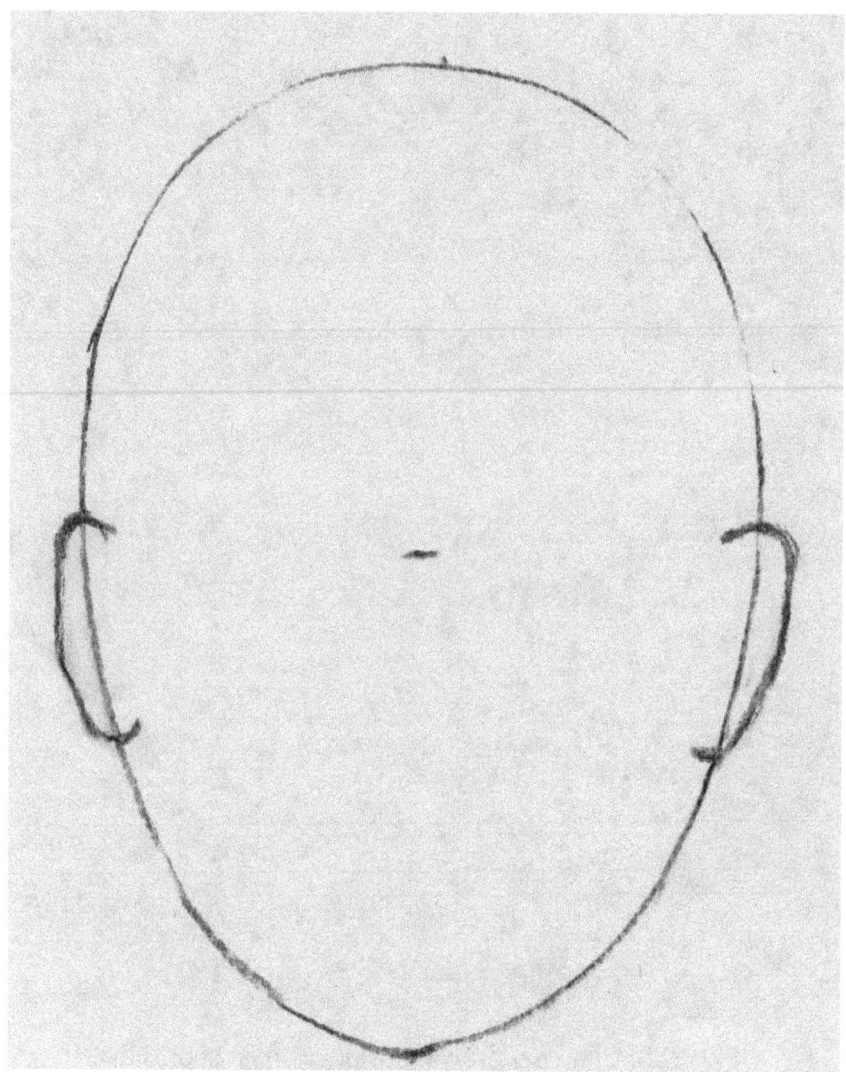

Fig. 24.

Step Two: Draw the outline of the hair

1. In this step, we will begin drawing the basic outline of the hair. Some of the hair will be drawn on the inside of the head shape and some will be drawn on the outside of it (see Fig. 25.) Continue to use your willow charcoal stick for this step.

2. Use your artist's eye to sketch in the placement of the general hair outline. Approximate how far down from the very top of the skull the hair line is in the centre of the forehead and make a small mark. It can be difficult to see the top of the head so we have to just guess at where it is. In general most hairstyles sit just a touch above the very top of the scalp. Refer to the photograph as a guide (see Fig. 23a.) The drawing is just an example.

3. Draw the shape of the hairline by using the mark as a guide. This part is very important and should be drawn as accurately as possible. The hairline plays a significant role (along with everything else) to determine the likeness of a person in a significant way. Take your time.

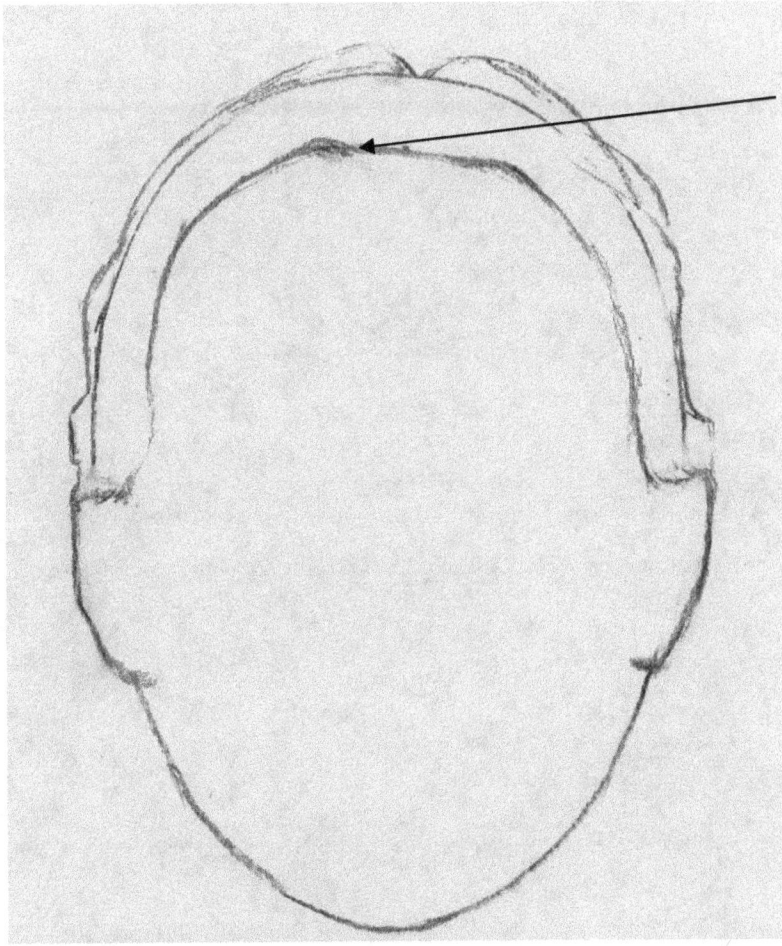

Make a mark to approximate how far down from the top of the skull the hairline begins.

Fig. 25.

www.DrawPJ.com

Step Three: Begin shading the dark tones

Seek out any prominent clumps of hair and draw these in, using your willow charcoal. There are some specific shapes that you will often use when drawing shorter and slightly wavy hair like we are here (see Fig. 26 inserts for examples.) Draw the outlines of these shapes first then fill in each end of the shapes with varying lengths of hatching strokes (still using your willow charcoal stick.) Leave the centres of these small pod-like shapes as the blank page ready for white charcoal later. Make up some of the markings but use the overall shapes and direction of the tones as a guide. Don't overdo the willow charcoal as this drawing will mostly be created with the white charcoal. Keep your lines and curves following the form of the general clumps of hair.

Short wavy clumps of hair are shaped like these. Practice on spare paper first to get the feel for these.

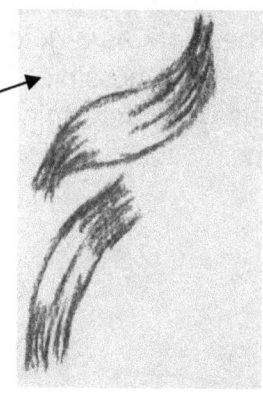
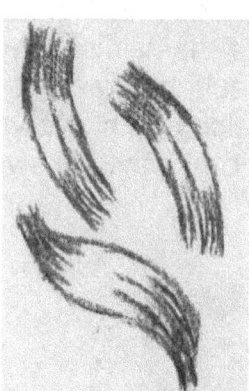

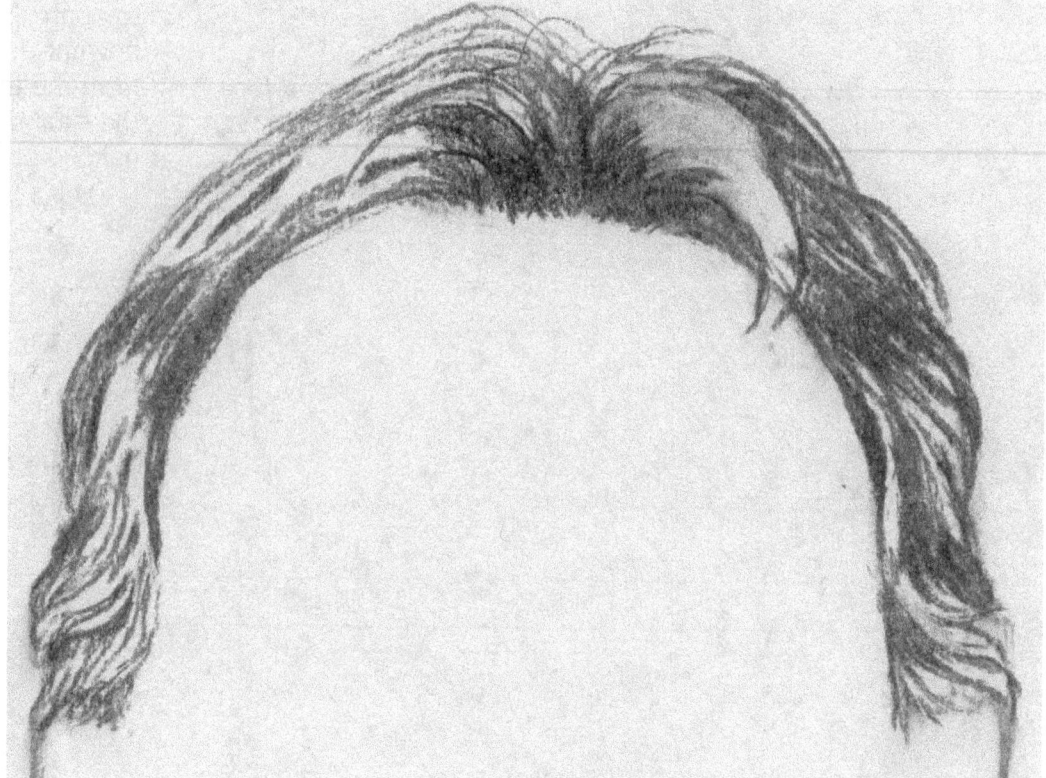

Fig. 26.

www.DrawPJ.com

Step Four: Blend the dark tones

1. Carefully blend the dark tones using your paper stump and follow the direction of the hair (see Fig. 27.) Do your best to retain the shapes of the individual clumps of hair and don't cover up the areas you left as the blank page. If you do, use your click-eraser to remove the charcoal again. At this stage you are still continuing to refine the general 'masses' of tone rather than drawing the individual hairs.

2. Shade a little area down onto the forehead using just the charcoal from your paper stump.

3. Use your putty eraser and click eraser to re-shape some of the highlight areas. Refer to your photograph continually (see Fig. 23a.)

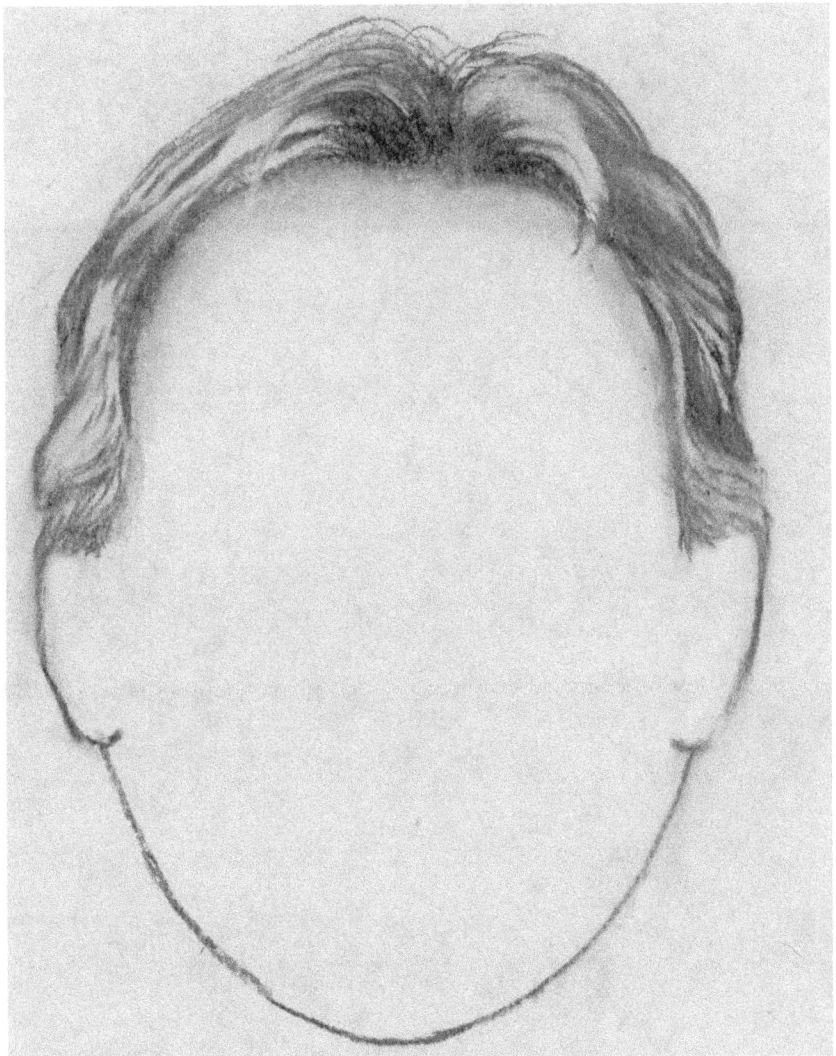

Fig. 27.

www.DrawPJ.com

Step Five: Add some individual dark hairs and white charcoal hairs

1. Refine the individual clumps of hair by hatching back into the dark areas using your 2B charcoal pencil. Retain the blank areas of the page carefully (see Fig. 28.) Do your best to refine the shapes of the individual clumps.
2. Add some very fine wispy hairs with your 2B charcoal pencil.
3. Add very fine white curved lines to the highlight areas including fine wispy hairs with your white charcoal.
4. You have competed the drawing.

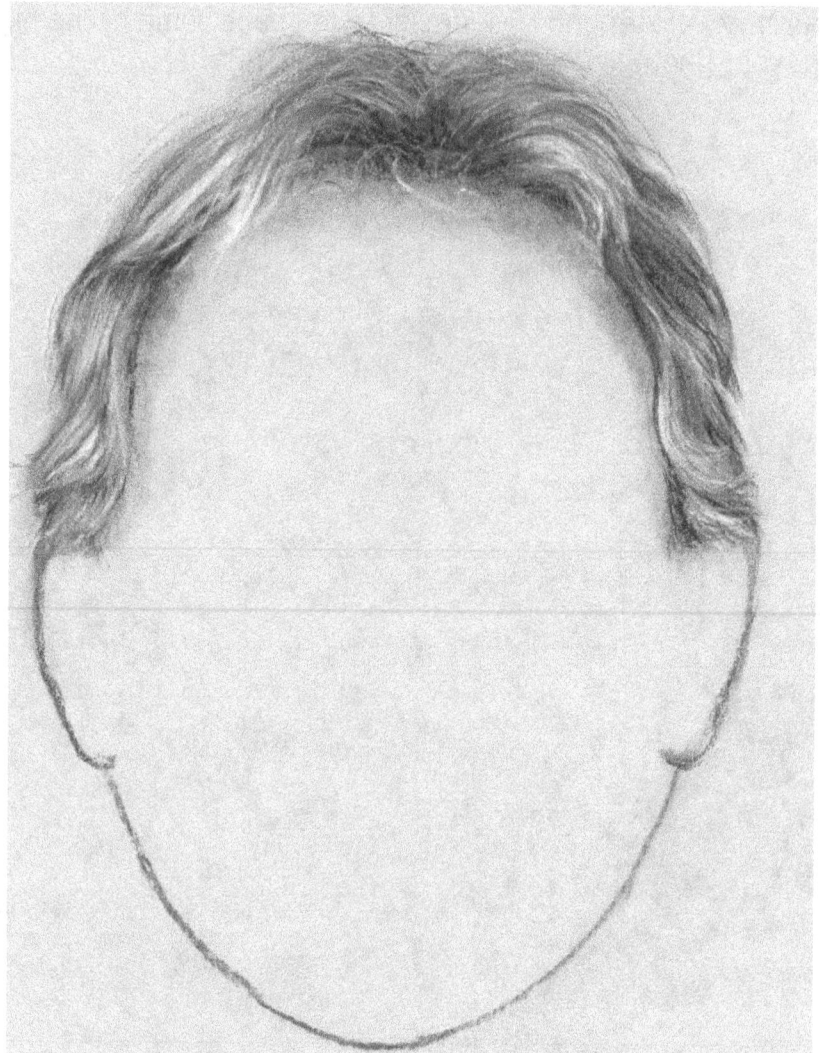

Fig. 28.

Step-by-step Instructions for Hairstyle Three: Adult Female Curly Hair

In this hairstyle example there is a lot of curly hair to draw with your willow charcoal and dark charcoal pencil. The hair will be drawn on the basic head template as mentioned above, with a neck shape added. Please use the photograph as your main reference source (see Fig. 29a) and the final drawing (see Fig. 29b) along with the other drawings as a guide for the step-by-step process. Work expressively and use your whole arm to draw. Refer to these drawings as often as needed. Make sure that you draw on the smooth side of a sheet of grey Mi-Teintes paper.

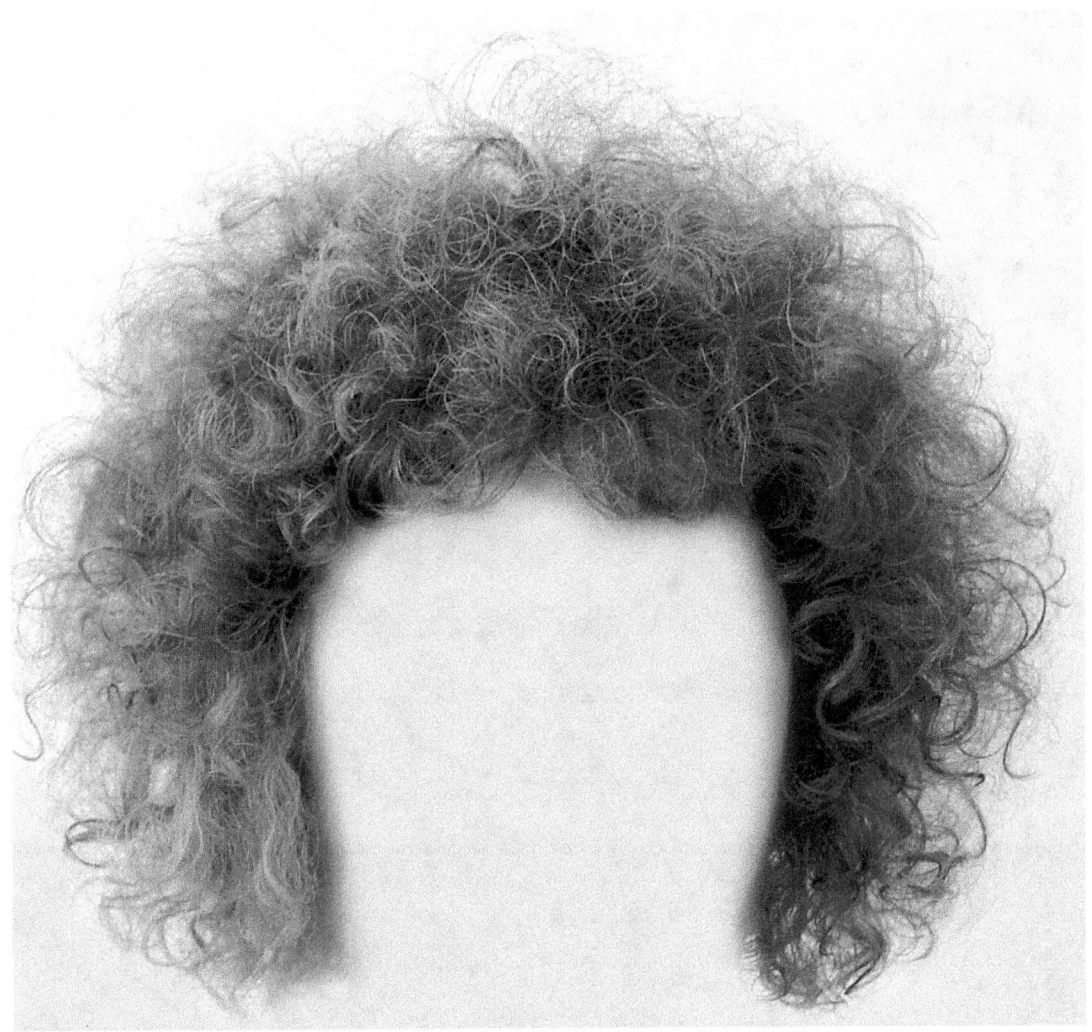

Fig. 29a.

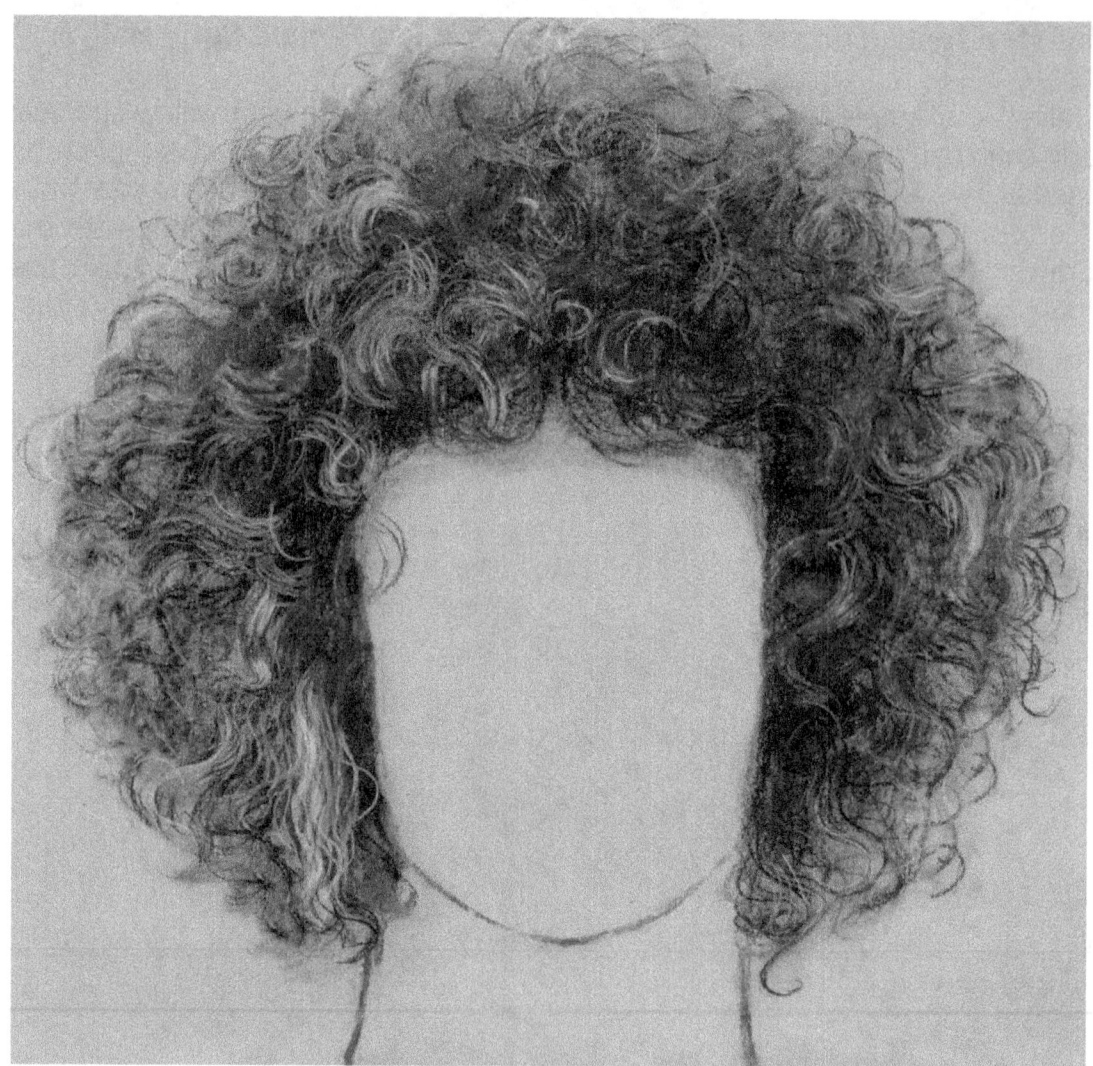

Fig. 29b.

Step One: Draw the head and neck shape

1. Begin by drawing the basic egg-shape for a head using the template as mentioned on page 33. Use your willow charcoal stick prepared with a chisel point to do all of your initial drawing with (see Fig. 30.) ***Resist the temptation to draw with your charcoal pencil*** as it doesn't blend or erase well. Save that until later in the drawing.
2. Draw in some curved lines to indicate the neck. Approximate the length and width of the neck. You can use the neck shape as a guide when drawing the longer parts of the hair by comparing your drawing to the one in your notes.

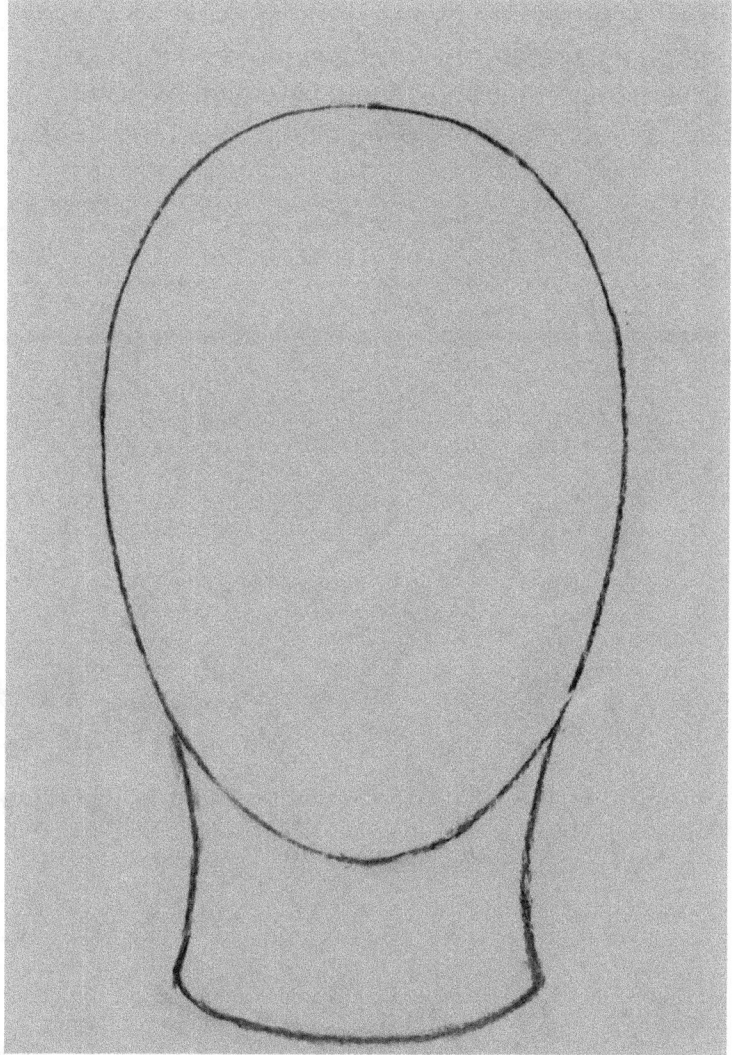

Fig. 30

www.DrawPJ.com

Step Two: Draw the outline of the hair

In this step, we will begin drawing the basic outline of the hair which ends just before the final tips of the hair end. The fine wispy tips of the curls will be extended out beyond this basic guide later. Some of the hair will be drawn on the inside of the head shape and some will be drawn on the outside of it (see Fig. 31.) Continue to use your willow charcoal stick for this step.

1. Mark in where the eye-line would be (half-way down the head.)
2. Approximate how far up from this mark centre mark the bottom of the fringe area ends and sketch in a line (see Fig. 31.)
3. Use your artist's eye to sketch in the placement of the major hair mass, using simple angles. Approximate by using the drawing as a guide (see Fig. 31) and the photograph as a reference for this part (see Fig. 29a.)
4. This part is very important and should be drawn as accurately as possible. The hairline plays a predominant role in helping to determine the likeness.

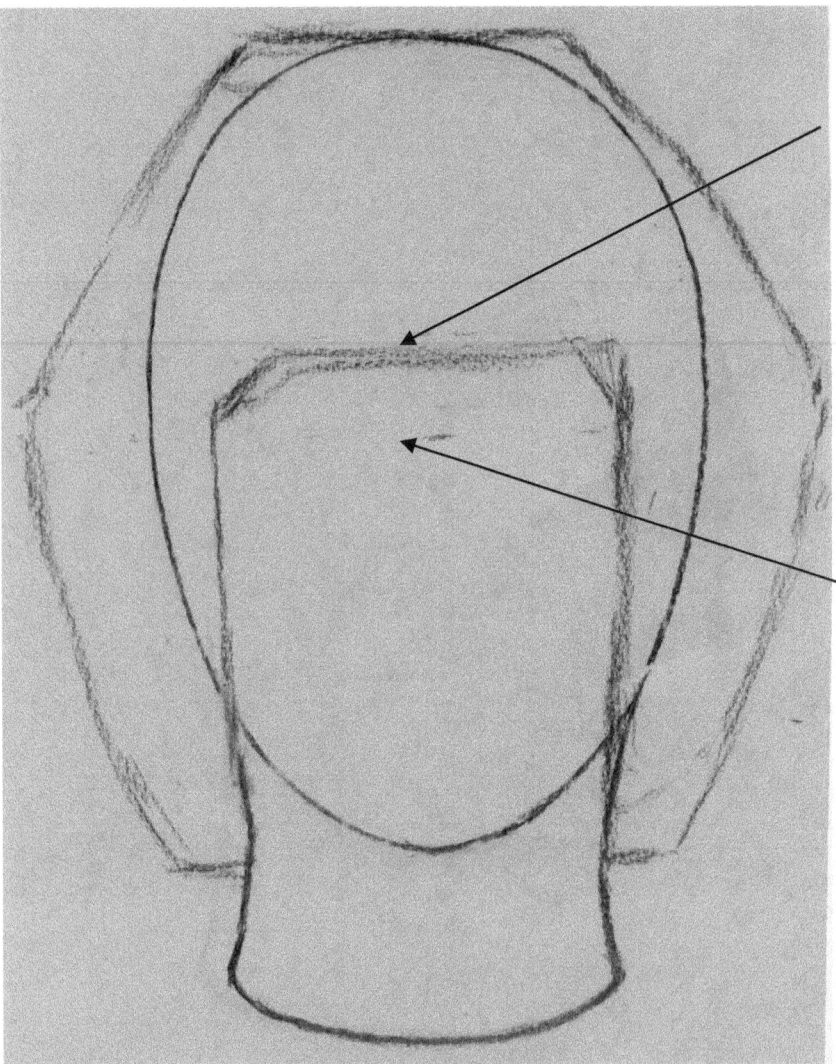

This line indicates the bottom of the fringe area (edge of the hair tips that fall across the forehead.)

This mark indicates the Eye level line ie: half-way down the full length of the head.

Fig. 31

Step Three: Begin shading the dark tones

Before you begin this initial step of the shading process, squint while looking at the photograph to see the darkest masses within the outline of the hair (see Fig. 19a.) Notice the overall mass is larger on the right side as the light source is coming from the left and lighting up the left side more.

1. Shade the dark shapes within the outlines that you have just drawn using a piece of a thick willow charcoal stick prepared with a chisel point. Use the large chisel shape mostly and occasionally the tip. Work in circular, scribbling motions. Press harder in areas that you see are darker and softer in others. Use your whole shoulder and elbow in the process, work confidently and expressively. Leave plenty of the page un-touched for later use (see Fig. 32.)

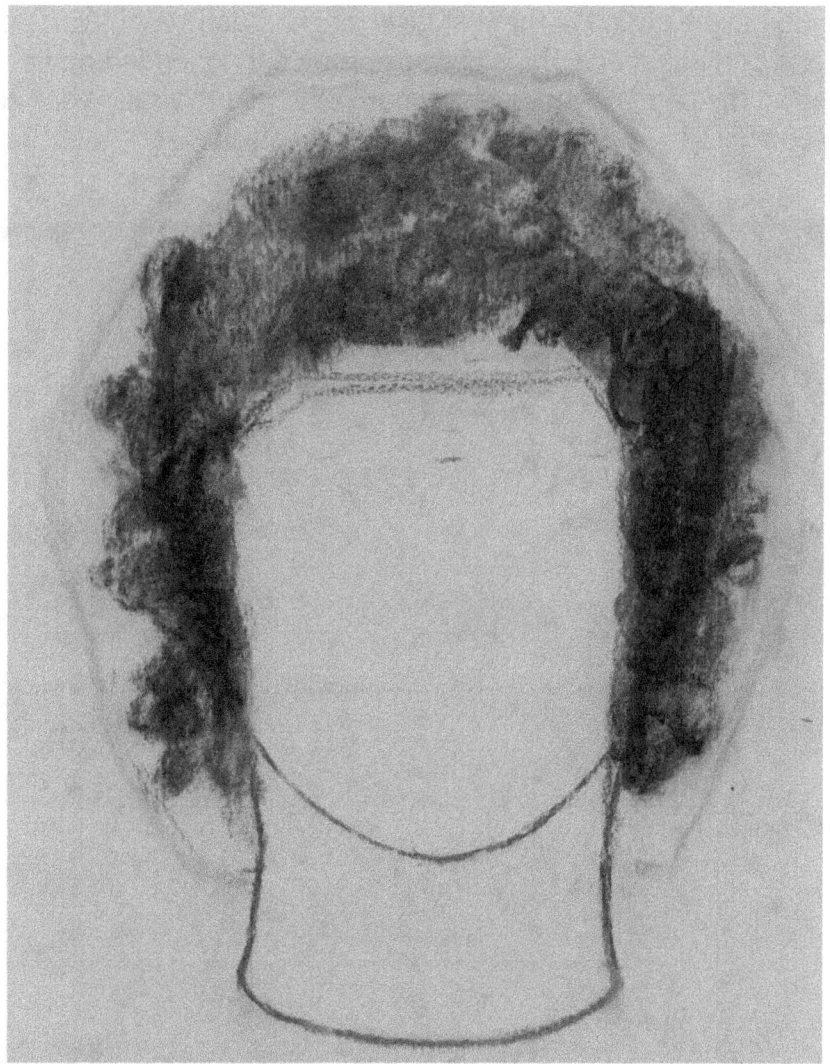

Fig. 32

 www.DrawPJ.com

Step Four: Blend the dark tones and add some curly hairs

In this step you will first of all blend the dark tones with your paper stump then place some squiggly and curly lines on top of those areas using your thin willow charcoal stick and your 2B charcoal pencil.

1. Using your paper stump and a circular motion do your best to retain the overall darker mass of the hair. At this stage you are still continuing to refine the general 'masses' of tone rather than drawing the individual hairs.
2. There are some specific wavy, curly-shaped lines that you will need to use for this type of curly hair as well as some generally large loose squiggly curves. See the individual curls in the photograph (Fig. 29a) as well as the insert here (see Fig. 33) then practice these on spare paper first using the tip of your thin willow charcoal stick prepared with a chisel point. It will wear down quickly needing continual preparation.
3. Once you have blended in the first layer of charcoal, scribble on many squiggly, wavy and curly-shaped curves over the top of the blended mass. Place on one layer using the point of your willow charcoal stick first, then your 2B pencil after that (see Fig. 33.) leave gaps in the squiggly strokes to retain the texture.

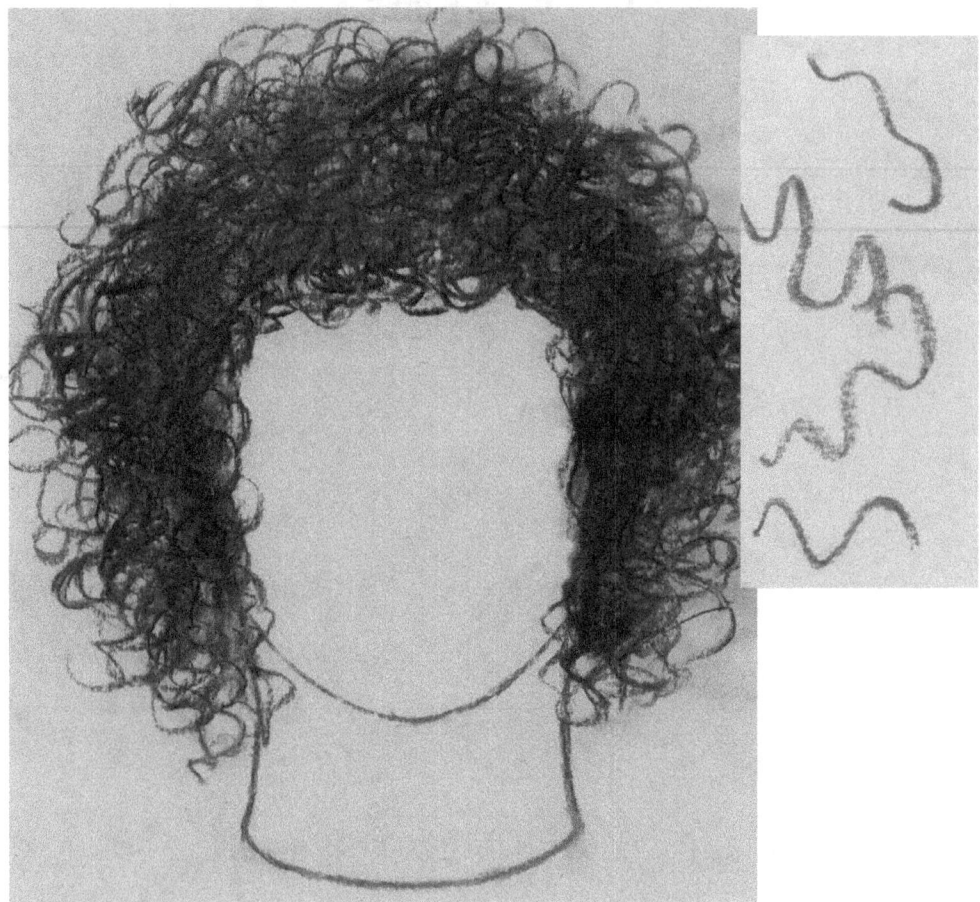

Fig. 33

www.DrawPJ.com

Step Five: Erase some areas for the highlights

Use the side edge of your gum eraser and occasionally your putty eraser to remove general areas of the charcoal ready to create some highlights. Please do not remove all the charcoal from these areas, you are just removing the loose charcoal and revealing parts of the page. Make sure that there are still some curly hairs just visible underneath. Stroke and pull your gum eraser to create the general shapes, curls and waves of the major highlight sections that you see in the photograph (see Fig. 29a.) and the drawing here (see Fig. 34.)

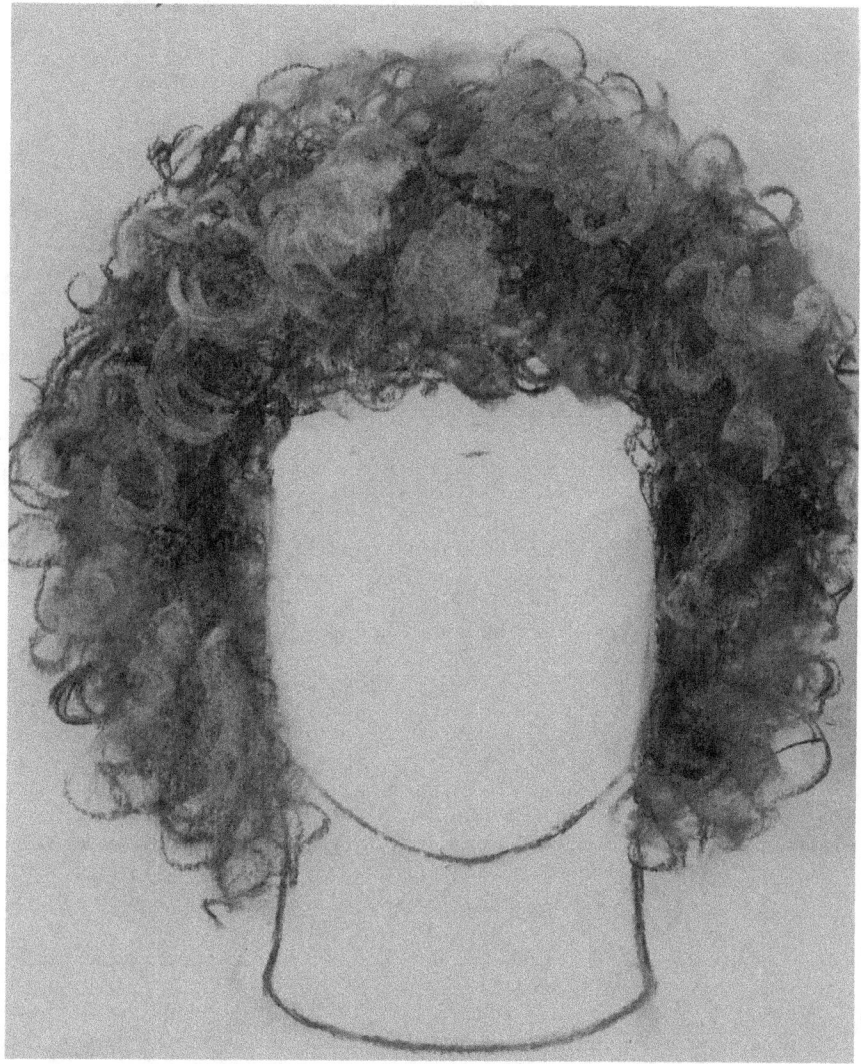

Fig. 34

Step Six: Erase some fine hairs

Use your click eraser with a sharp tip. You need to cut the tip of the click eraser quite often to achieve the thin lines for hair. Continue to refer to the photograph to draw in some curly wavy marks with the corner of the tip on your click eraser (see Fig. 35.)

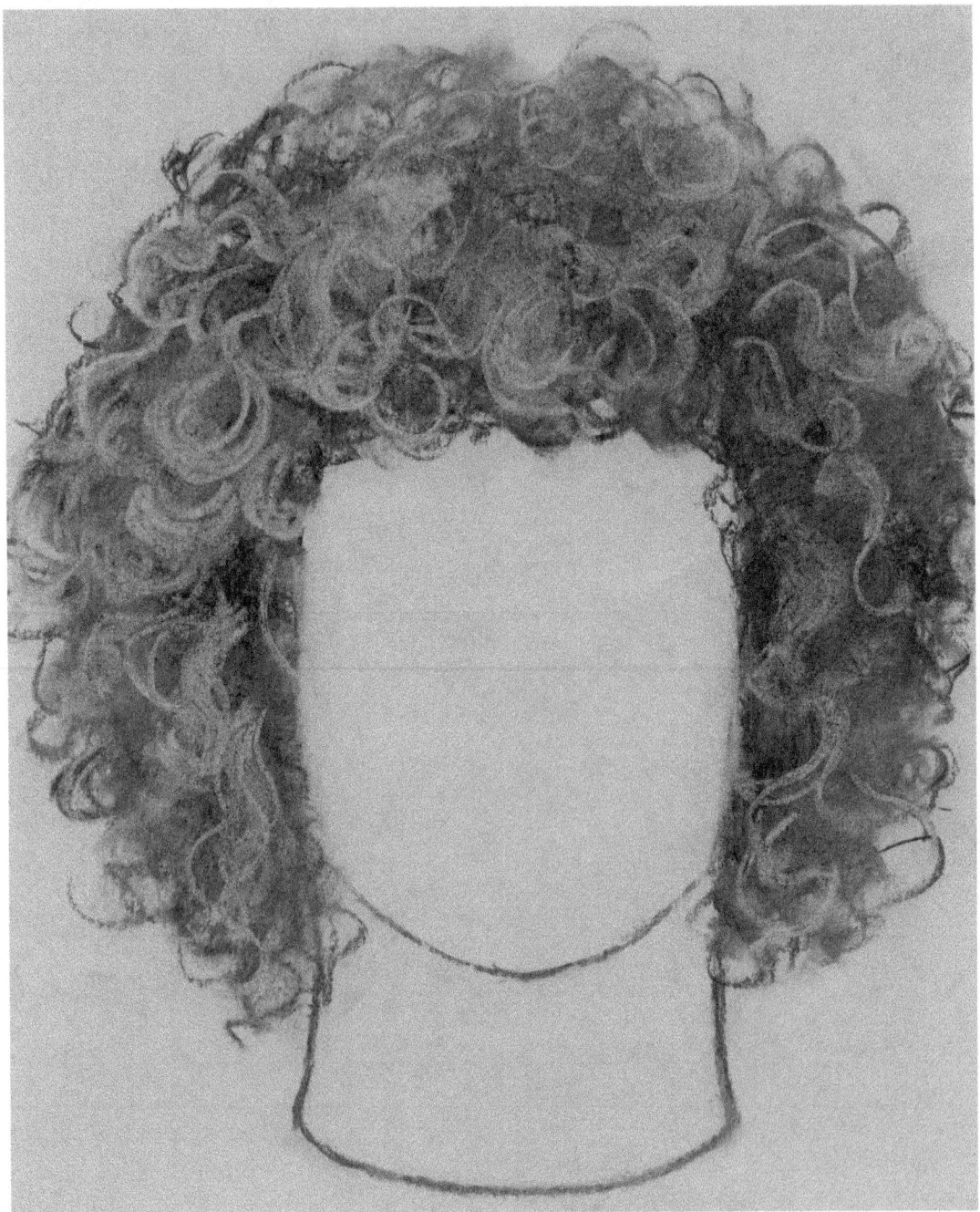

Fig. 35

www.DrawPJ.com

Step Seven: Add some individual clumps of dark hairs

In this step you need to refine the individual clumps of hair by hatching some fine curves into the dark areas using your sharpened 2B charcoal pencil. Retain the highlight areas carefully (see Fig. 36a.) Do your best to refine the shapes of the individual clumps by **_hatching on either side of the curl_** as well as on either ends of each clump. Take careful note of the placement of the major clumps (see Fig. 36b.) You have to squint hard to see these and look for a while at the photograph. Concentrate hard until your creative brain kicks in to help you do this.

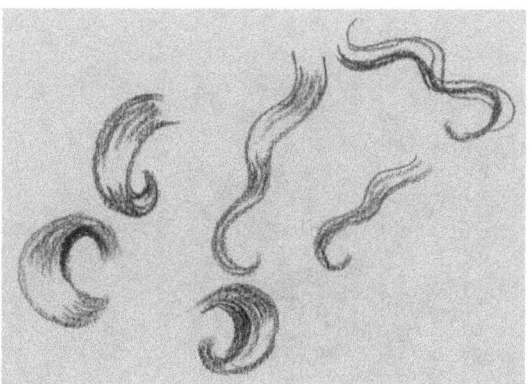

Fig. 36a. examples of clumps of curls with hatching

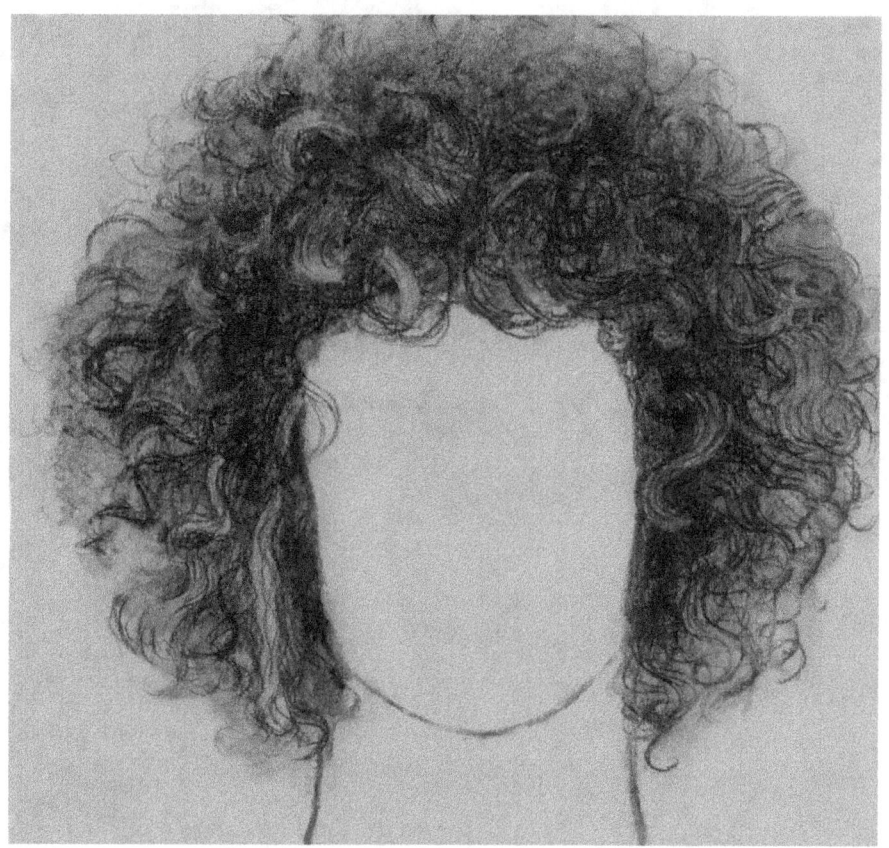

Fig. 36b.

Step Eight: Add some fine highlighted hairs

1. In this final step you need to further refine the individual clumps of hair by hatching some fine curves and waves using your ***white charcoal*** pencil. Look constantly at the photograph (see Fig. 29a.) and then at the drawing here for ideas (see Fig. 37.)

2. Once you have finalised this step, your curly hair is complete!

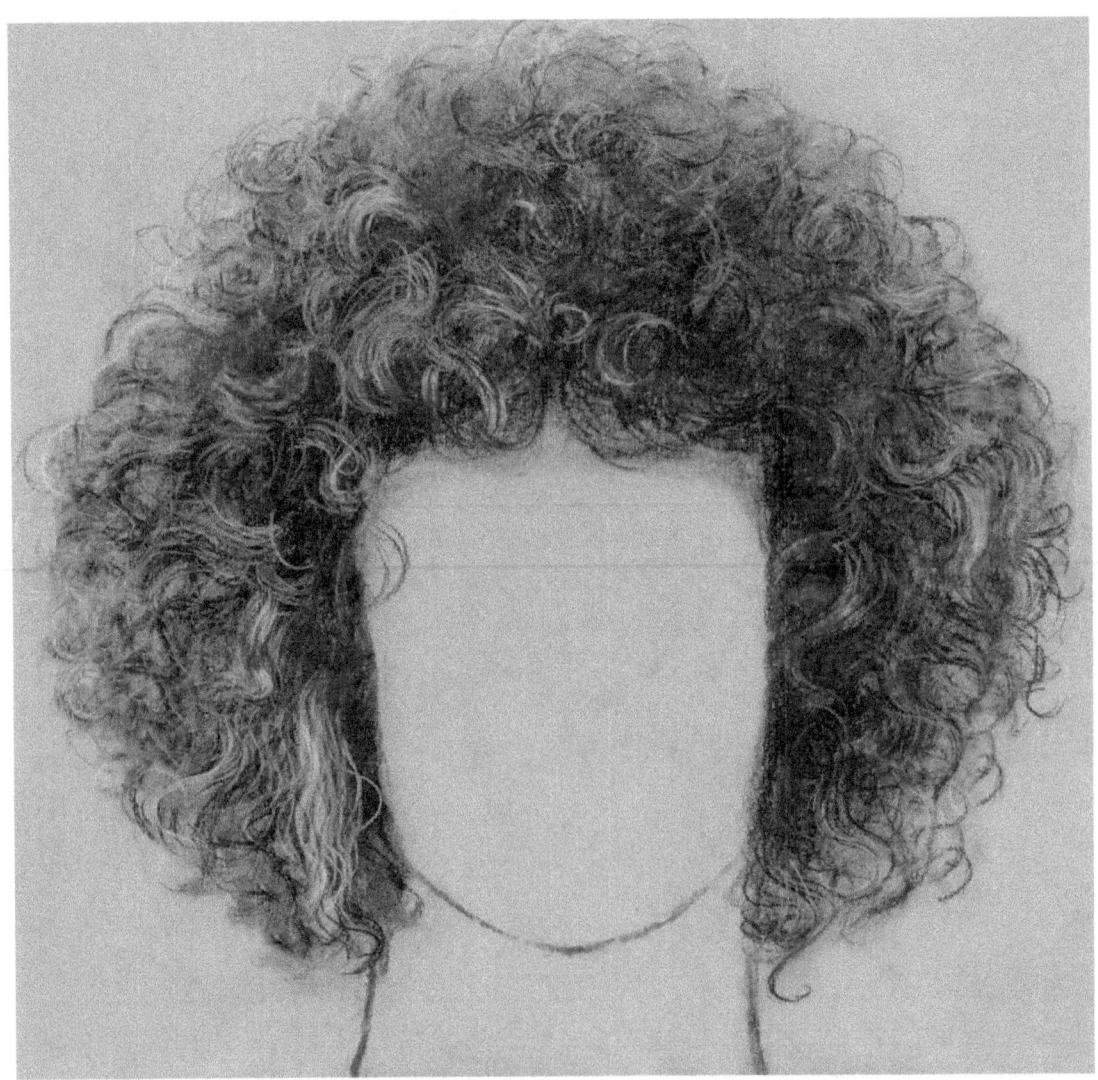

Fig. 37

www.DrawPJ.com

Tip: Charcoal is a fascinating medium like no other. It can work almost like a chalk board. This is not always good though, especially if you manage to smudge a wonderful almost-completed piece of artwork.

You can minimize this risk by placing a sheet of non-waxy baking paper under your hand at all times or better still, a piece of 'Glassine' which is a slippery piece of see-through paper you can purchase from an art supply store. We also use this special paper to cover the front of the charcoal images for protection while storing.

Also, be sure to spray your image once you are happy with it but always photograph your work before you spray. You can use hairspray but it can yellow over time and finding the right one is tricky. Its best to invest in a can of professional fixative for pencil and charcoal from your local art supply store.) Read the instructions on the can very carefully, it can make a huge mess on your artwork if you spray too close or too much at once. The spray can dribble down the paper if you are not careful. To avoid accidents test the spray on a sheet of scrap paper first.

Summary for week two

Your course this week involves a lot of individual techniques. There is a lot to learn with charcoal, however, you are sure to find it an immensely rewarding and easy medium to use once you have been shown how. If there was one major piece of advice that we could give in summary about charcoal, it is this; "Less is best!" In other words when you think you have to put on more charcoal or make it 'look better' think twice. Stop working on the image before you think you must.

Charcoal really is easier than it looks and that can be hard to believe! Keep it simple and you will do well. Resist the urge to 'over-do' your drawings. Lay the charcoal on then leave your drawing alone, don't fiddle. Try to see the overall picture rather than getting too bogged down in the little details. Charcoal is not a great medium for tiny details. It is at its best when you use it with expression and a looser approach to drawing.

Charcoal is a wonderfully forgiving, creative medium. Embrace the wonderful qualities of charcoal with excitement and your work will reflect that positive energy. After all, like all drawing activity, charcoal drawing is a reflection of the soul.

Remember to 'Just show up at your table' and the rest will take care of itself! Have a fun week.

Week Three

Introduction to week three

During this week you will have the opportunity to further explore the diverse qualities of charcoal as you refine the skills learned in the first and second weeks of the course. You will call upon your knowledge of the 12 different charcoal techniques and it's a good idea to refer to your sheet of these techniques as often as needed.

You will be asked to begin by selecting just one of the objects to draw first, then continue on until you have created all three drawings. You will be using charcoal and white Conté on light grey Mi-Teintes paper. There are larger images provided for you to print out on quality paper at the beginning of each step-by-step process. These three different objects provide a variety of textures which will allow you to practice the charcoal techniques needed for your final portrait drawing next week.

Exercise for week three: Draw the objects provided

Begin this exercise by selecting just one of the three objects to draw first. You will see a photograph and then alongside the photograph is an example of the completed charcoal drawing (see Figs. 38a and 38b, Figs. 39a and 39b, Figs.40a and 40b.) Please read about how each of these different textures can help you to practice for your final portrait drawing in the section titled 'Relevance Of These Textures to Portraiture.'

Once you have made your selection please continue to the section of your choice where you will be taken step-by-step through the process of creating the drawing in charcoal. Before you begin creating any of these exercises please draw a six tone value scale in willow charcoal at the top or bottom of your page.

Please use the photograph as your main reference source. The images provided are an example of the process suggested to use.

Relevance Of These Textures to portraiture

Large Urn:

This drawing of the Large Urn will help you to refine your light and shade skills as well as give you more confidence with charcoal drawing in general (see Figs. 38a and 38b.) It is ideal for practicing shading larger areas with simple shadows. Although the urn has a more rugged texture than the skin in a face normally would, the light and shade skills that you access here, are the same skills that are required for drawing the shadow shapes in the face and neck areas of your portrait.

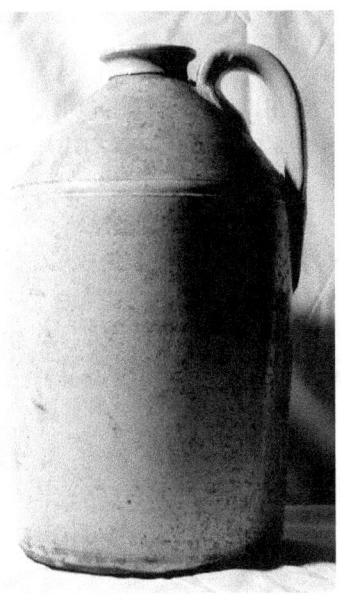
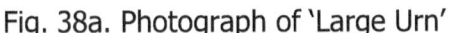
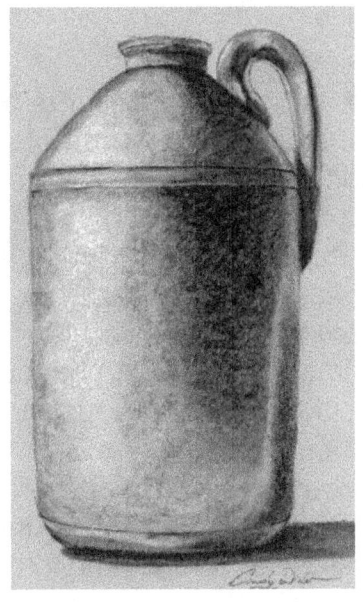

Fig. 38a. Photograph of 'Large Urn'   Fig. 38b. Drawing of 'Large Urn'

Old Wooden Post:

This drawing will help you gain confidence and skills that are required to draw many subjects (see Figs. 39a and 39b.) The variations in thick and thin lines coupled with shadows and highlighted areas provide you with similar techniques that you will also call upon when drawing hair.

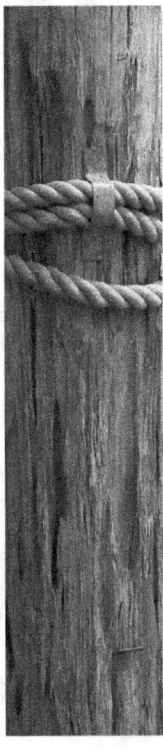
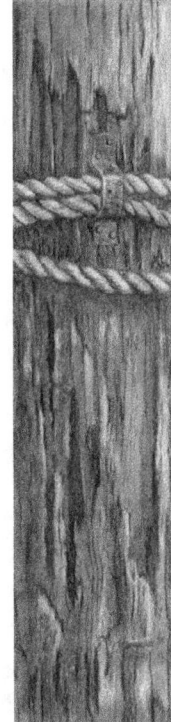

Fig. 39a. Photograph 'Old wooden Post'   Fig. 39b. Drawing 'Old Wooden Post'

Drapery:

This exercise will give you a chance to practice drawing folds (see Figs. 40a and 40b.) Many times, when you are drawing a portrait you might find yourself choosing to include fabric in some shape or form.

Drapery is another term for 'cloth in use.' It is wise to practice drawing basic drapery as the knowledge you gain can be adapted to many other subjects as well. This drapery example will give you the opportunity to practice some of the techniques needed to draw folds that can be found in a shirt, piece of material draped around a person's shoulders or other upper-body garments.

The methods used here also apply to drawing the rolls or folds of skin in a mature or chubby person's neck area. The skin has different shapes to the cloth, but the same techniques are used to draw the folds in skin.

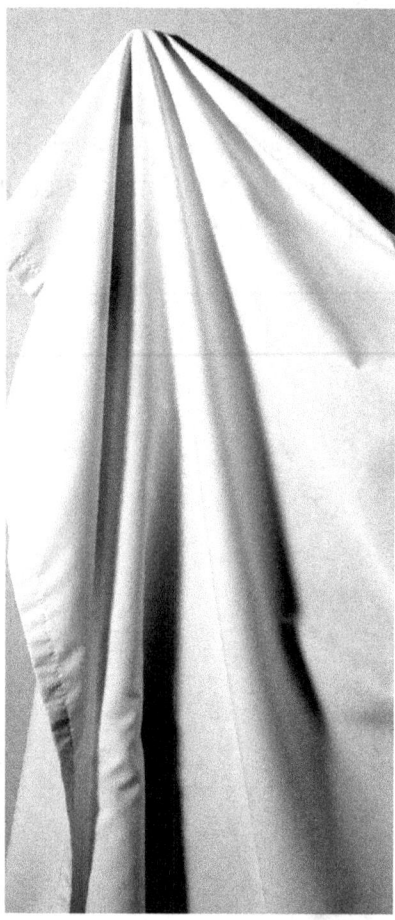
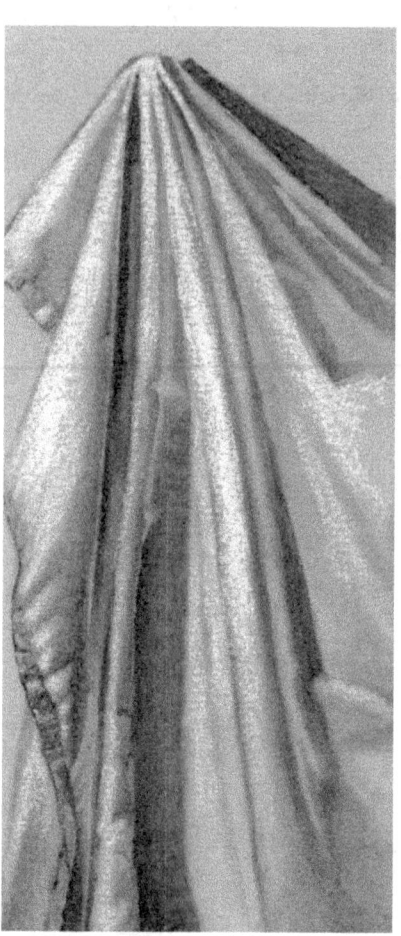

Fig. 40a. Photograph 'Drapery'   Fig. 40b. Drawing 'Drapery'

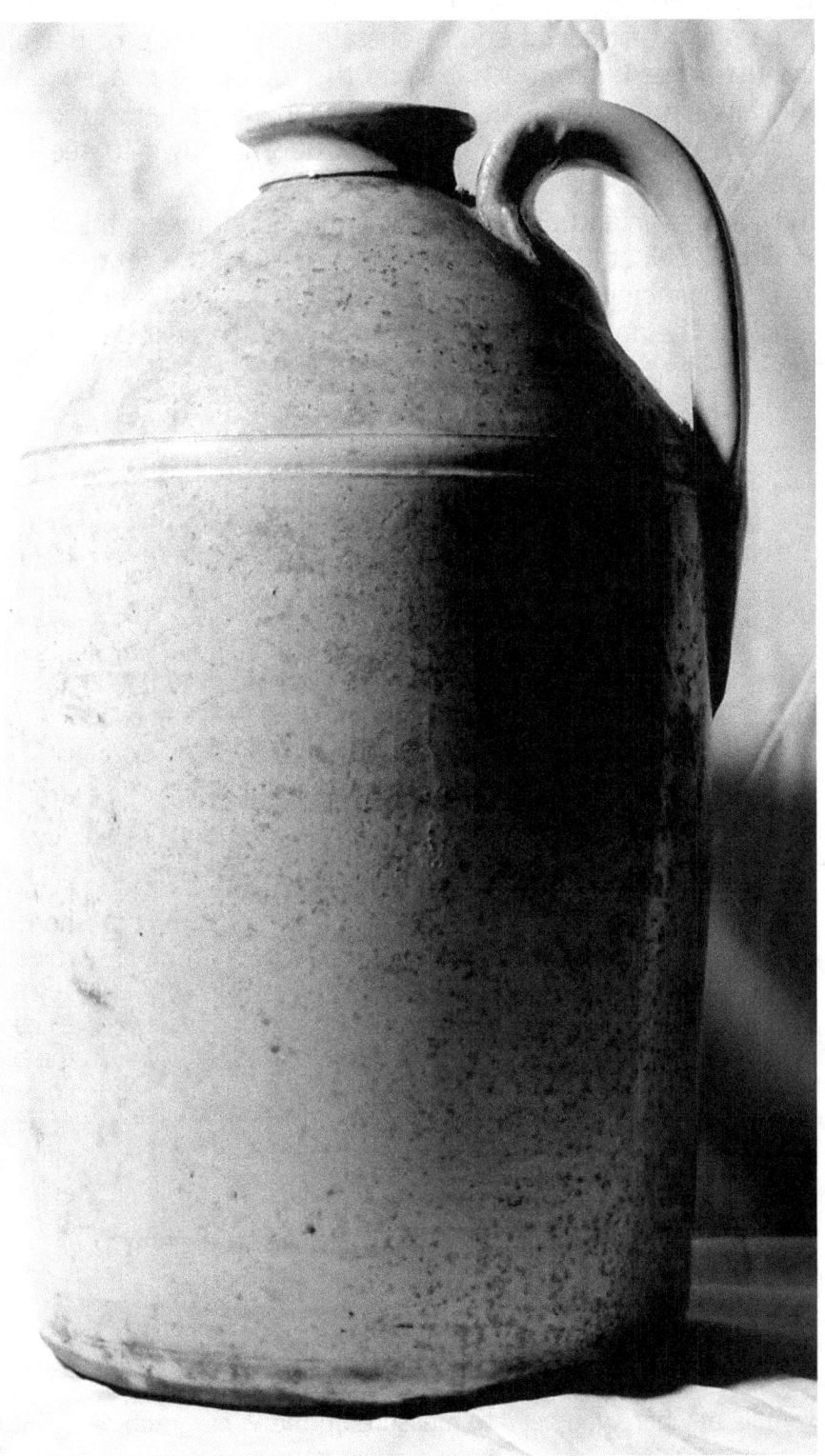

Fig. 41. Photograph of 'Large Urn'

Step One: Make some measurements on a clear plastic sheet

1. Print the photograph; 'Large Urn' onto photo-quality paper (see Fig. 41.)
2. Place a sheet of clear plastic or acetate over the top of the photograph you have just printed and attach it along the top of the image with tape. You will be drawing on this sheet with a fine permanent marker. Attaching it only to the top allows you to lift the plastic sheet up and down to see the image more clearly when needed.
3. Using your ruler and fine permanent marker draw on the clear plastic sheet (see Fig. 42.) First of all rule a vertical line down the centre of the *main body* of the urn beginning at the very tip of the top lip and ending at the base. Do not include the handle in your measurements. This will be measured separately later.

A vertical line is first of all drawn onto the sheet of clear plastic covering the photograph. This line is drawn down through the middle of the object and measured from the very top to the very bottom of the urn. See the blue arrows.

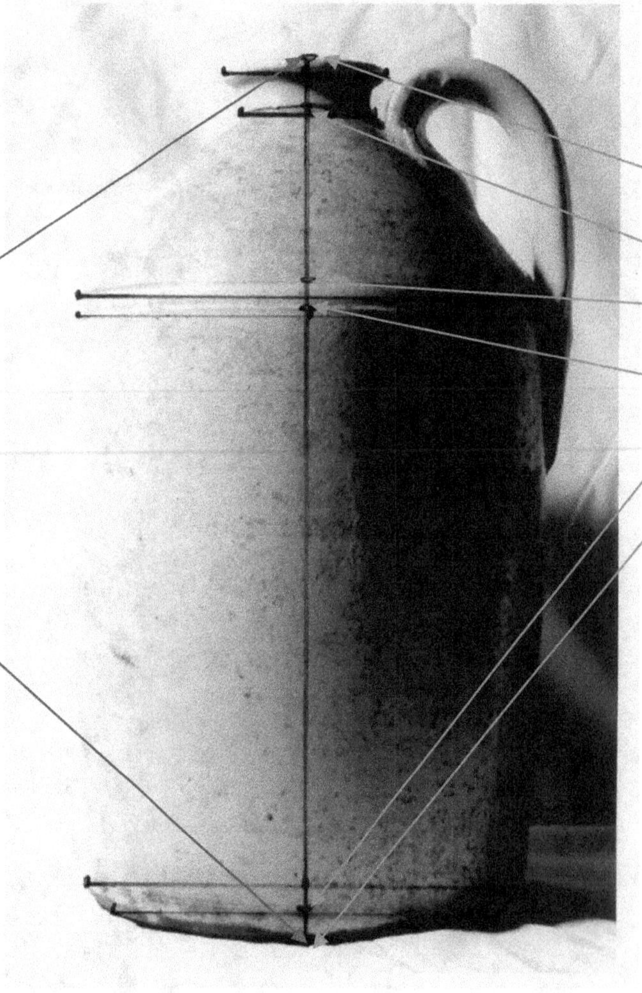

Once the centre vertical line is drawn onto the sheet of clear plastic, then short lines (dashes) are placed to mark the full height of every ellipse down along the vertical line. See the red arrows.

Finally, the horizontal lines are ruled through the centre of each ellipse. These are the black horizontal lines you can see drawn onto the urn. Make sure these are even on either side of the vertical line.

Fig. 42. Example of where you need to measure on the Photograph of 'Large Urn'

Note: The images provided are not drawn to the same size as the photograph in Fig. 41. Please refer to Fig. 41 for all of your measurements.

4. Once you have ruled the centre vertical line, begin at the top end of the urn and place a short line (dash) to mark the position of the full height of every ellipse you see (see Fig. 42.)

5. Rule horizontal lines through the centre of every ellipse. You can see these lines ruled in black on the photograph (see Fig. 42.) Make sure you measure the width of each of these lines very carefully to check that they are even on either side of the vertical line. This is to make certain that your vertical line is indeed in the exact centre.

Step Two: Begin drawing on your Mi-Teintes paper with charcoal

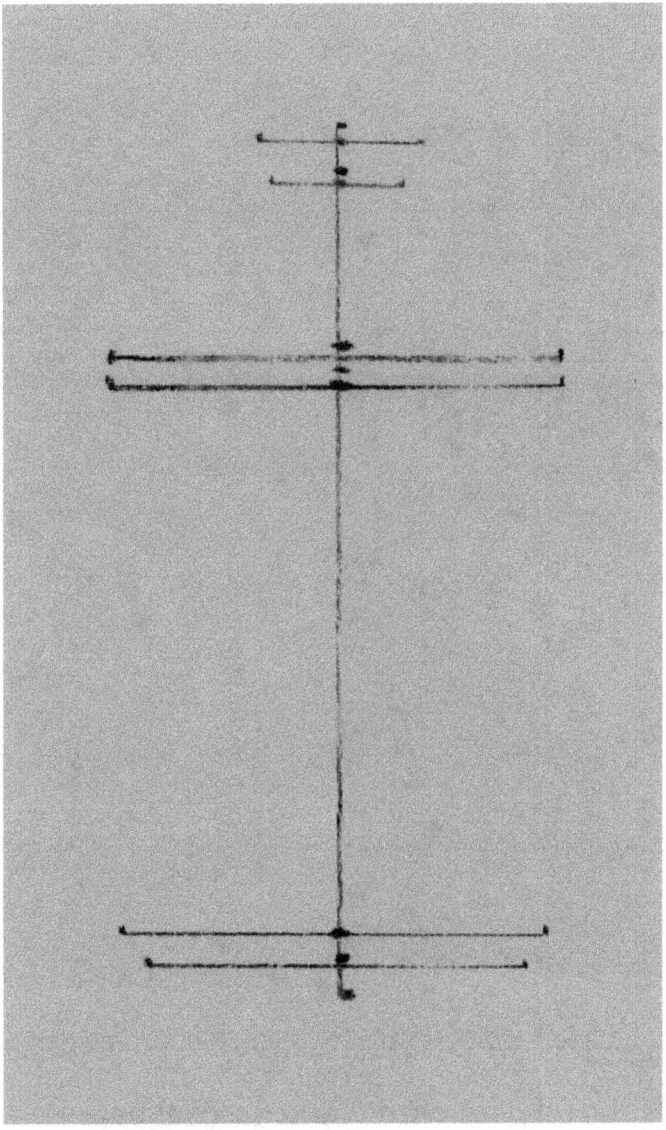

Fig. 43. Example of the first drawing on your Mi-Teintes paper using willow charcoal

Tip: Place your black permanent marker well out of reach for a short while because you must not accidentally use it on your Mi-Teintes paper.

1. After you have measured and ruled the basic guidelines onto your clear plastic sheet covering the photograph, you can then draw the same size and placement of these lines onto the **smooth side** of your Mi-Teintes paper (see Fig. 43.) Use the very tip of your **willow charcoal stick** prepared with a chisel point *(note: do not use your charcoal pencil for your guidelines as it is difficult to erase.)*

2. Once you have drawn the basic guidelines onto your paper, go back to your clear plastic sheet covering the photograph. Continue to draw the rest of the outline drawing onto the clear plastic sheet (see Fig. 44a for an example.) Then draw the same shapes onto your paper over the top of the charcoal guidelines you drew previously (see Fig. 44b.)

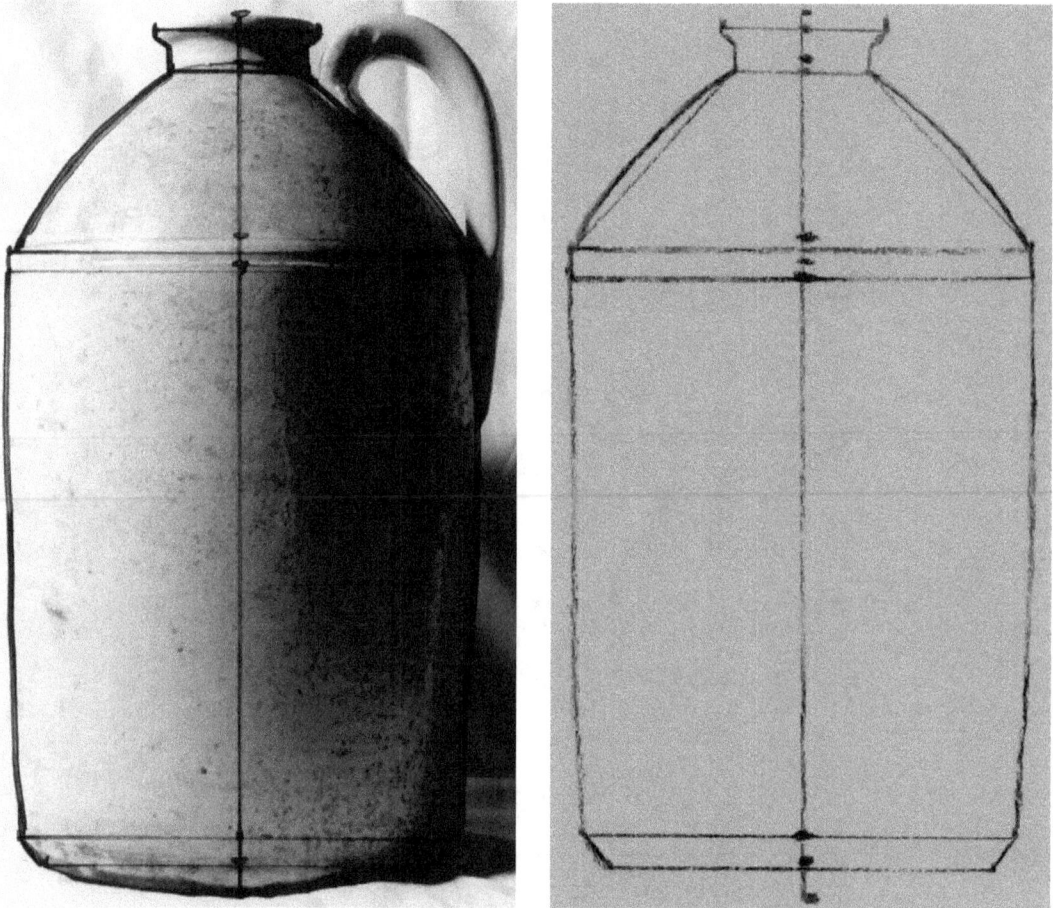

Fig. 44a. Example of outline drawn over photo   Fig. 44b. Example of outline drawing

Step Three: Draw the ellipses onto your charcoal paper

Take careful notice of where the ellipses need to be drawn on and make sure that you draw them as gentle curves like you see in the drawing provided. You can draw the full ellipse then erase the part you don't need. For an example of ellipses drawn with just the front curves see Fig. 45. Ellipses must be drawn accurately to be convincing.

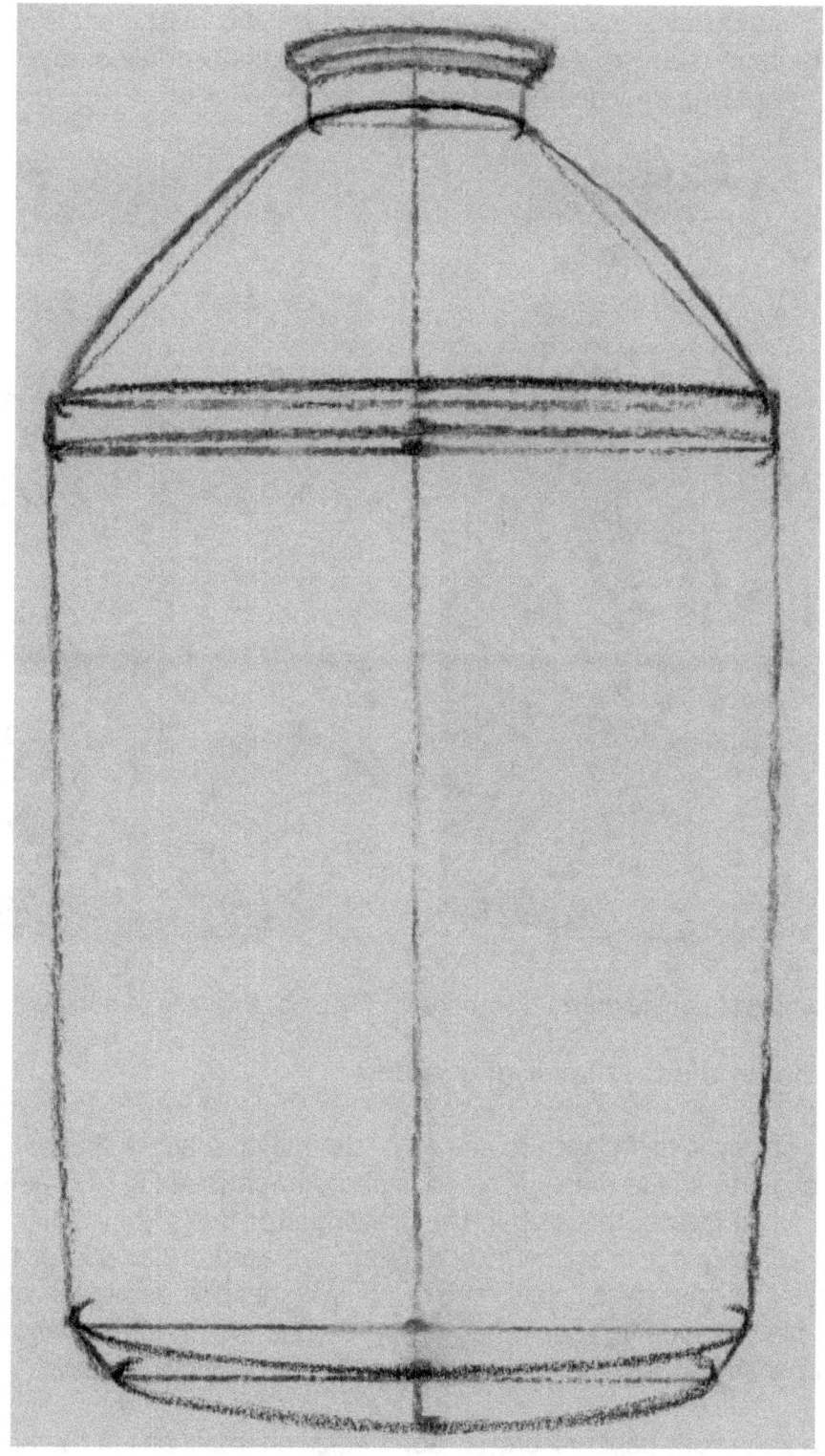

Fig. 45. Example of the ellipses drawn onto the construction outline drawing

www.DrawPJ.com

Step Four: Draw the construction outline for the handle

Take notice of the construction guidelines used here to draw the handle (see Fig. 46a.) Measure and draw these basic lines and shapes on the plastic sheet covering the original photograph (see Fig. 41) before drawing the final curves onto your paper as you see in the drawing provided here (see Fig. 46b.)

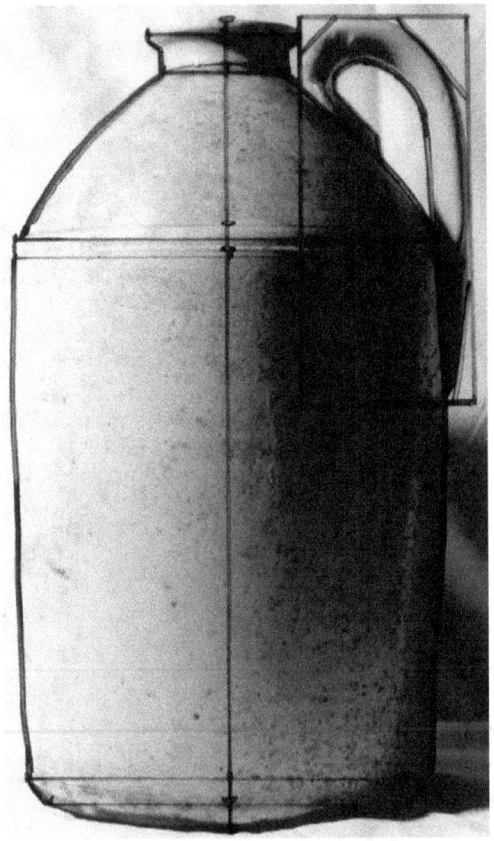 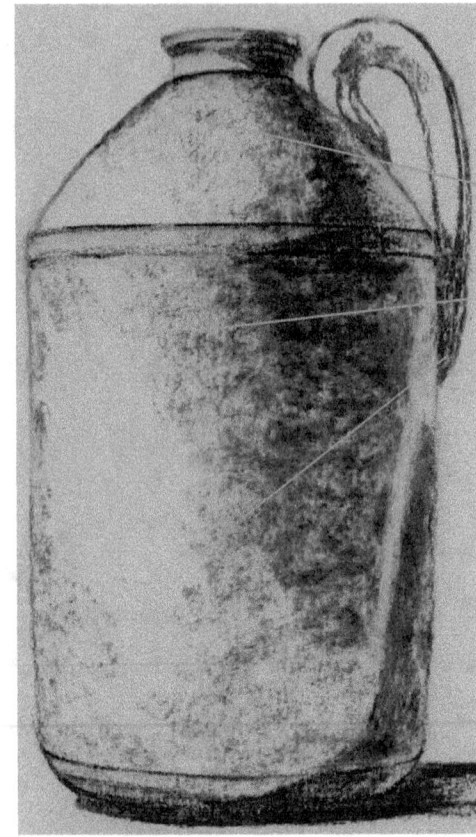

Press lightly with your charcoal to leave a lot of the paper exposed in between the speckled patches of charcoal to create your level 3 tones

Fig. 46a. Example of outline drawn over photo   Fig. 46b. Example of outline drawing

Step Five: Begin the first layer of shading

Squint with your eyes half-closed to see all of the major shadow shapes (the darkest areas) and begin to shade these using your photograph (see Fig. 41) as a guide and the drawing as an idea of this step in the drawing process (see Fig. 46b.) Shade the areas using a thick piece of willow charcoal either placed on its side or by using the large flat area of the chisel point stroke. If you need a reminder of these two techniques, please refer to your notes for week one on; *1. Cover large areas with willow charcoal and, 2. Cover medium-sized areas with willow charcoal.*

Be careful to keep your paper clean (ie: don't place charcoal on) in the areas that are your number 1 and 2 tones. Press very lightly with your charcoal to leave a lot of the paper exposed in between to create a speckled effect for your level 3 areas of tone (see Fig. 46b.)

Step Six: Blend this layer with your paper stump

Once you are satisfied with the general placement of the large shadow shapes and highlight areas that are left behind as the blank page, blend the darkest areas in carefully with your paper stump. Leave some sections un-touched in the level 3 areas to create texture and then reapply a little more charcoal afterwards using the softest possible touch. This will add more texture. Do your best to maintain the shapes of your major shadow-edge areas, keep your paper clean in the areas that will become the number 1 and 2 levels (see Fig. 47.)

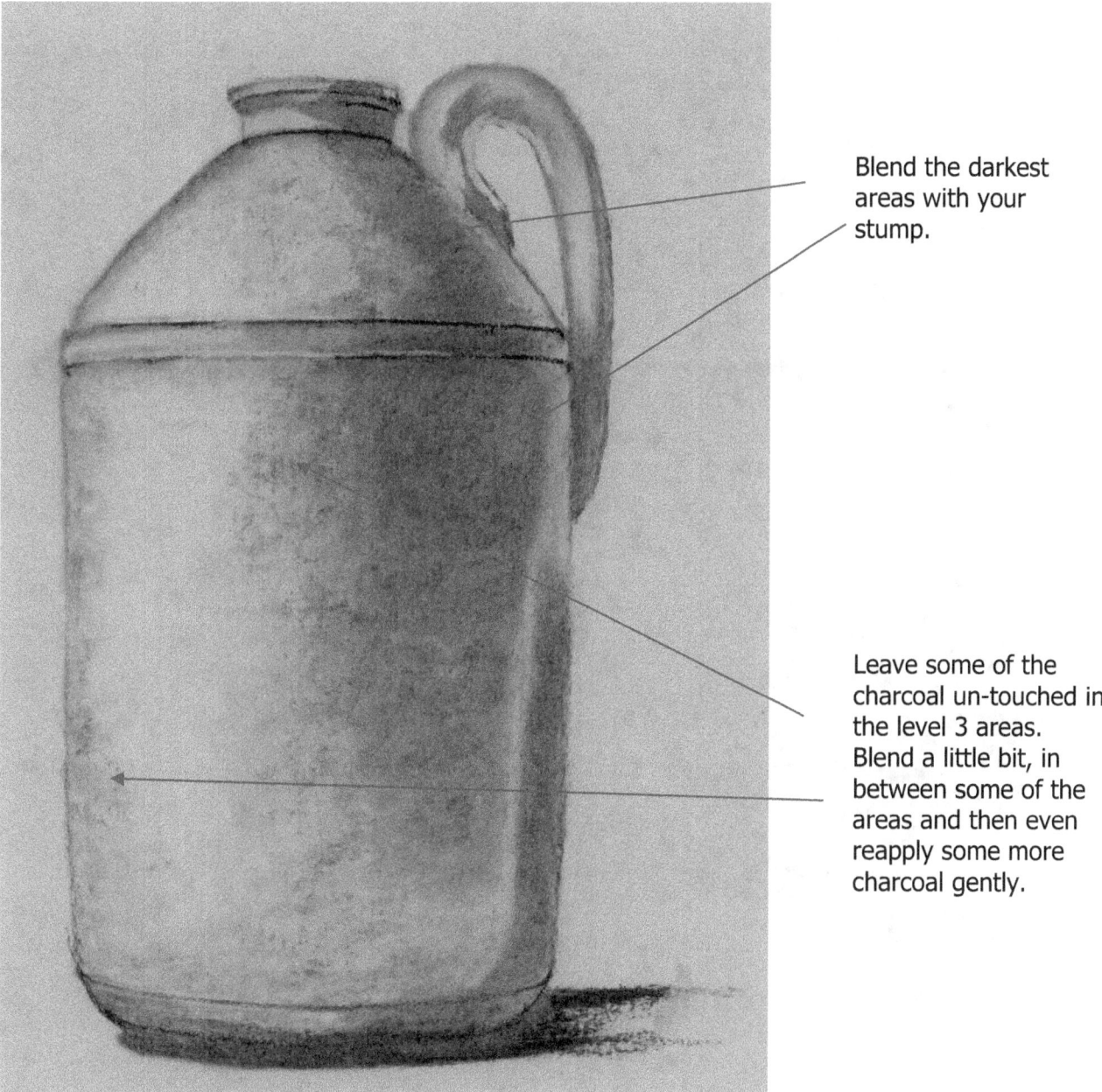

Blend the darkest areas with your stump.

Leave some of the charcoal un-touched in the level 3 areas. Blend a little bit, in between some of the areas and then even reapply some more charcoal gently.

Fig. 47. Blend the darkest areas and leave some of the charcoal untouched in the level 3 areas to create texture

Step Seven: Add some more charcoal to create texture and depth

Now it is time to really darken the shadow edge area as well as add more texture. This step is fun and you can really get your elbow involved here. Use a combination of your willow charcoal with the large area of the chisel point flat on your page and your *2B charcoal pencil*. Apply a scribbling motion into the level 4, 5 and 6 tones as shown in the insert here (see insert Fig. 48.)

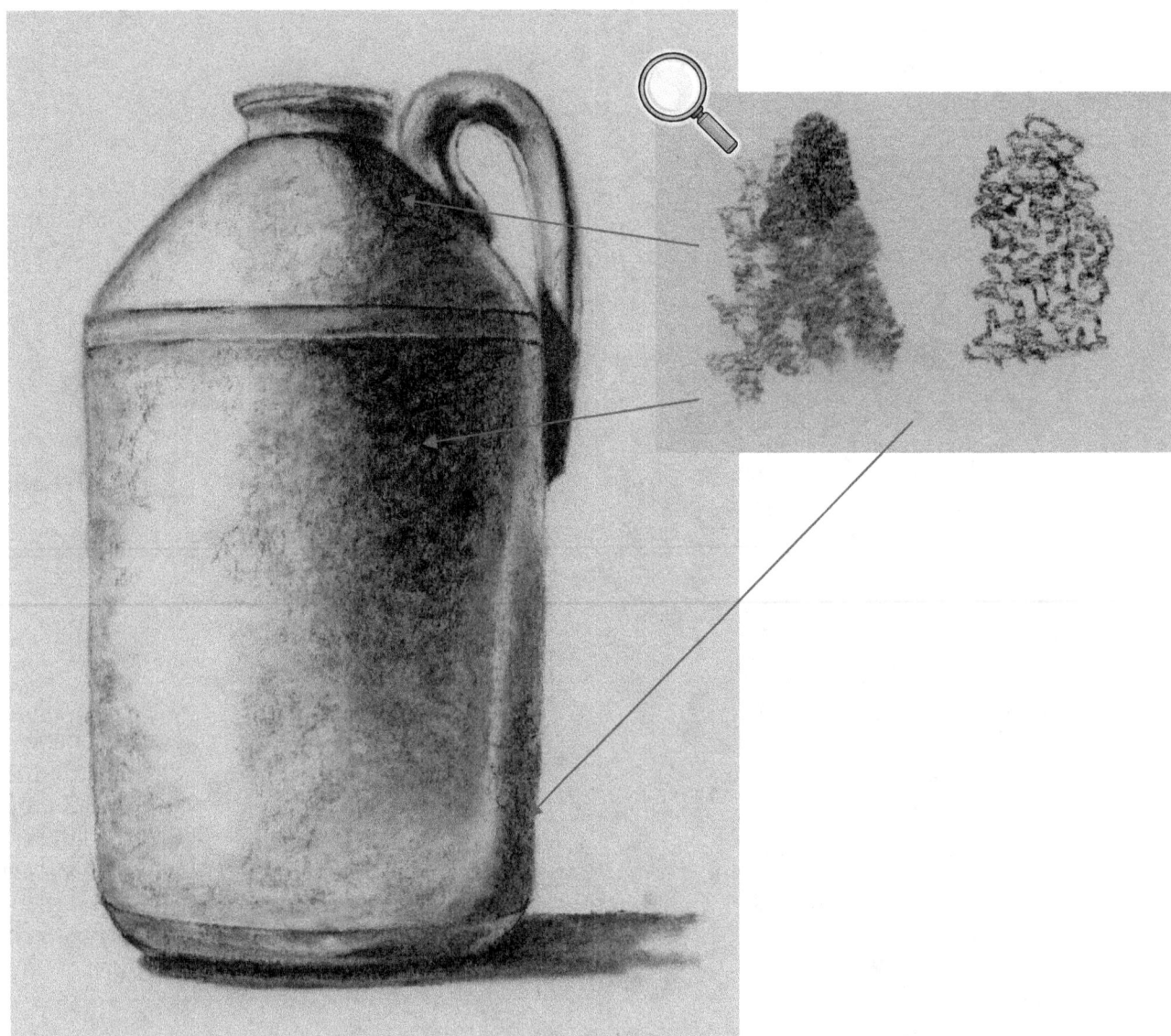

Fig. 48. Darken the tones in the shadow edge areas and create more texture

Step Eight: Add white Conté as a finishing touch

The final touch simply requires some white Conté placed into the areas you have left as blank page. You don't need to fill the entire area. Lay a small piece of the white Conté on its side and drag it back and forth across the number 1 full light areas. Press harder to achieve slightly more solid areas in the centre of the highlight (see Fig. 49.) Use the tip to highlight the small areas along the lip of the ellipses and the handle.

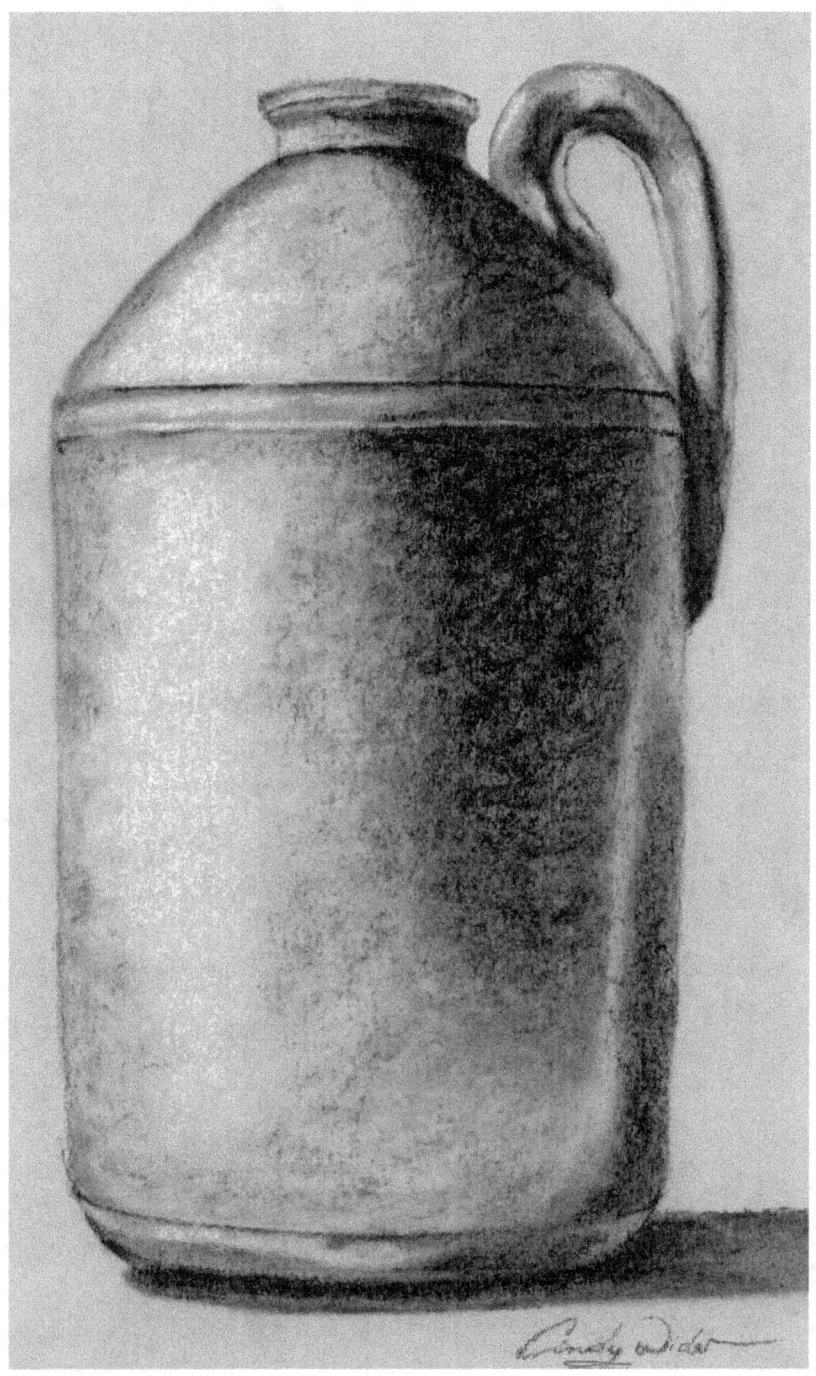

Fig. 49. Add the white Conté in the number 1 full light areas for a finishing touch

2. Step by Step Old Wooden Post

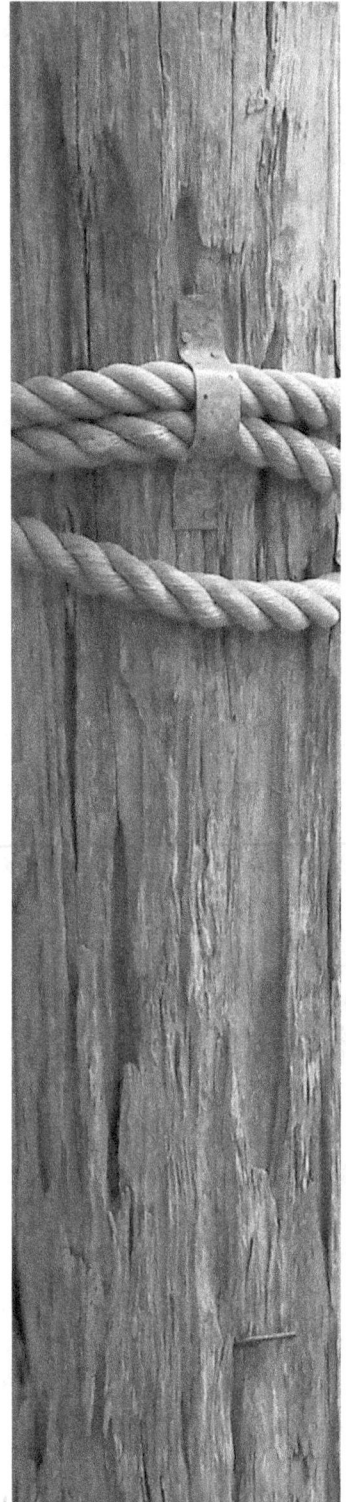 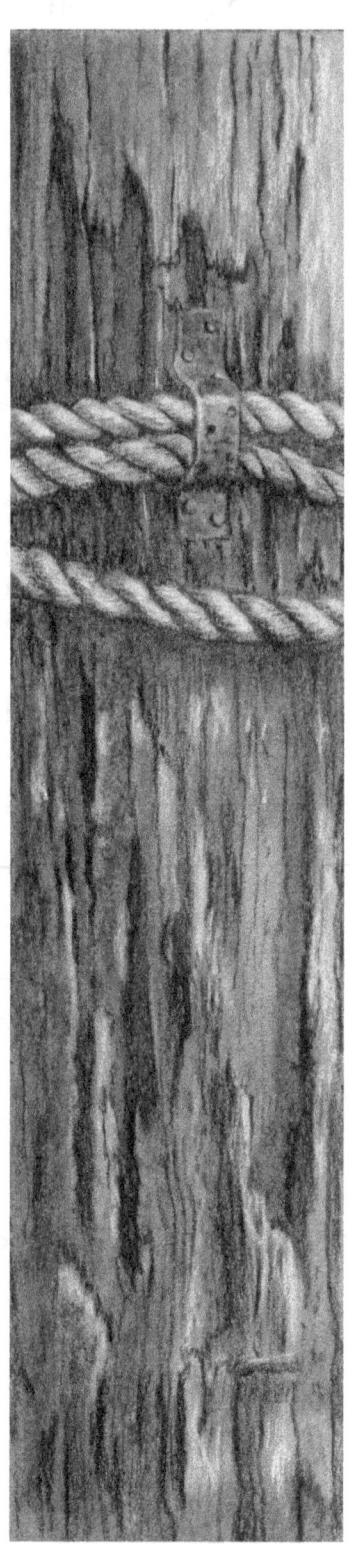

Fig. 50a. Photograph of 'Old Wooden Post'   Fig. 50b. Drawing of 'Old Wooden Post'

www.DrawPJ.com

Step One: Draw the outline then shade the background

1. Use the tip of your thin willow charcoal stick prepared with a chisel point and your ruler to draw a rectangle (20cm x 4.5cm) on the **smooth side** of a sheet of pale grey Mi-Teintes paper. Refer to the photograph in your notes as your main reference source (see Fig. 50a.)

2. Copy the simple outline drawing of the three ropes and clip that holds the ropes to the post. Use the photograph to measure from (see Fig. 50a) and the drawing as a guide to indicate what shapes to draw (see Fig. 51a.) You can draw the shapes more accurately by using your ruler to measure the distance of the objects from the top or sides of the rectangle. You could begin by measuring how far down the top of the rectangle the clip is positioned, then how far it is from the left side. Make small dashes to mark the positions of each part of the clip then draw the simple outline as shown in the example (see Fig. 51a.)

3. Once you have completed the outline drawing, begin shading the background area behind the rope and clip using the large ellipse area of a thick piece of willow charcoal prepared with a chisel point.

4. Shade the area darker on the left as you see here (see Fig. 51b.)

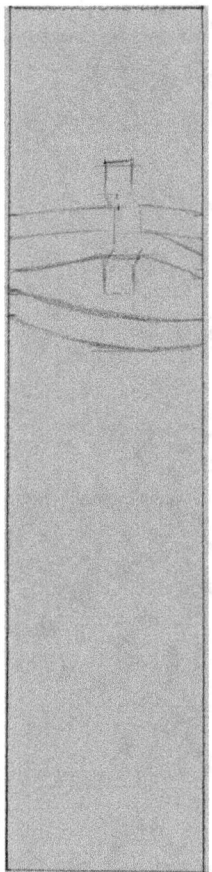

Fig. 51a.

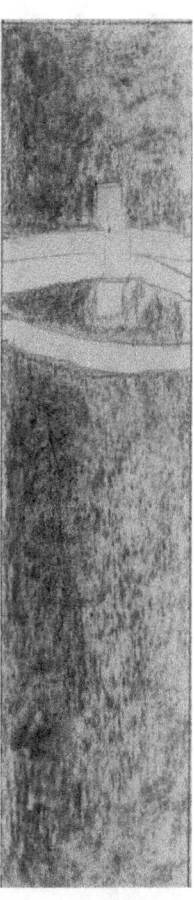

Fig. 51b.

StepTwo: Blend the background with your paper stump and begin the textured areas

1. Use your large paper stump to carefully blend the background area. Do your best to keep the left side darker than the right side.
2. Begin to apply the textured wood grains using fine jagged lines with lots of variety (ie: thick and thin areas) with a very sharp **2B charcoal pencil** (see Figs. 52a and 52b.) Seek out all the major shapes in the wood and draw these (refer to Fig. 50a.) Only work in the area above the ropes. We will gradually be making our way down the wooden post completing each area as we go to reduce the possibility of smudging.
3. Draw the outline of each segment on the ropes making sure you place tiny curves along the outside of the rope (see the insert Fig. 52a.)
4. Draw a half circle around the small nails in the clip and a dark line along the entire left side of the clip. Lightly shade the clip with your paper stump and some loose charcoal powder.

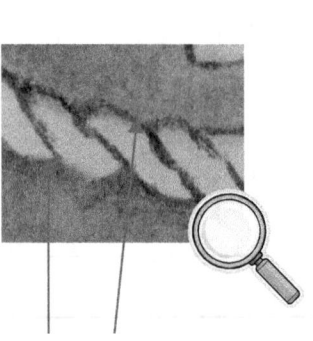

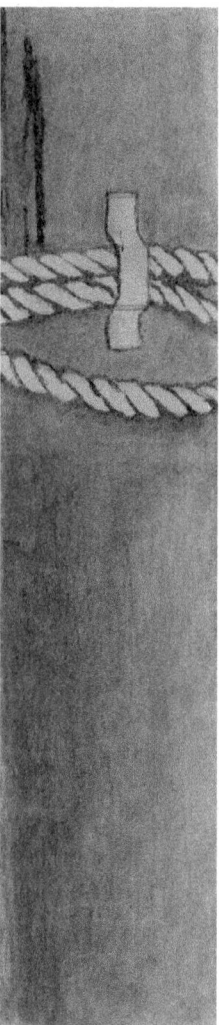

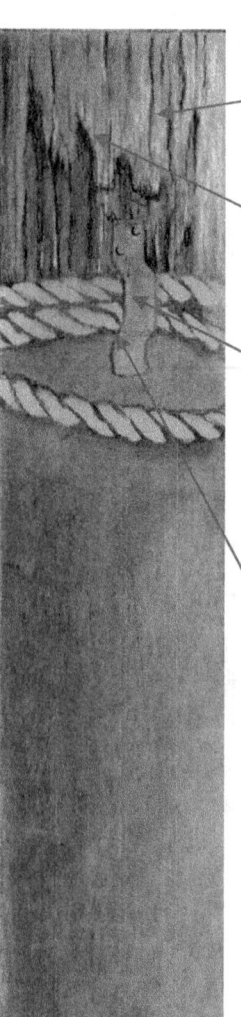

Draw the outline of the ropes. Make sure you draw the little curves along the sides of the ropes and each individual segment carefully.

Count how many segments there are before the clip and after as a proportion guide.

Putty back some areas for highlights.

Apply some white Conté in these areas.

Shade a soft layer onto the clip using your paper stump and loose powder.

Draw a dark line along the left side.

Fig. 52a.   Fig. 52b.

1. Once you have drawn the major dark areas of the wood pattern you can then use your putty eraser to lighten back the highlight areas of the wood (see Fig. 52b.) Always refer to the photograph as well as the drawings provided and make your own decision on what areas you see need highlighting (Fig. 50a.)
5. Apply some tiny amounts of white Conté to the highlight areas that you have just erased to give the wood more of a three-dimensional appearance. Complete this area (see Fig. 52b.)

Step Three: Add some texture to the ropes and clip

1. Use a sharp *2B charcoal pencil* to draw some very fine, curved hatching lines on the left side of each of the tiny sections of rope (see the insert in Fig. 53.)
2. Using a sharp white charcoal pencil, draw fine hatching lines on the right side of each little section of the rope (see the insert in Fig. 53.)
3. Add some small circular shapes to the metal clip with the tip of your fine willow charcoal stick (see insert Fig. 53) then gently blend some of these with your paper stump. This creates the texture of beaten metal. Remove any highlights with a putty eraser.

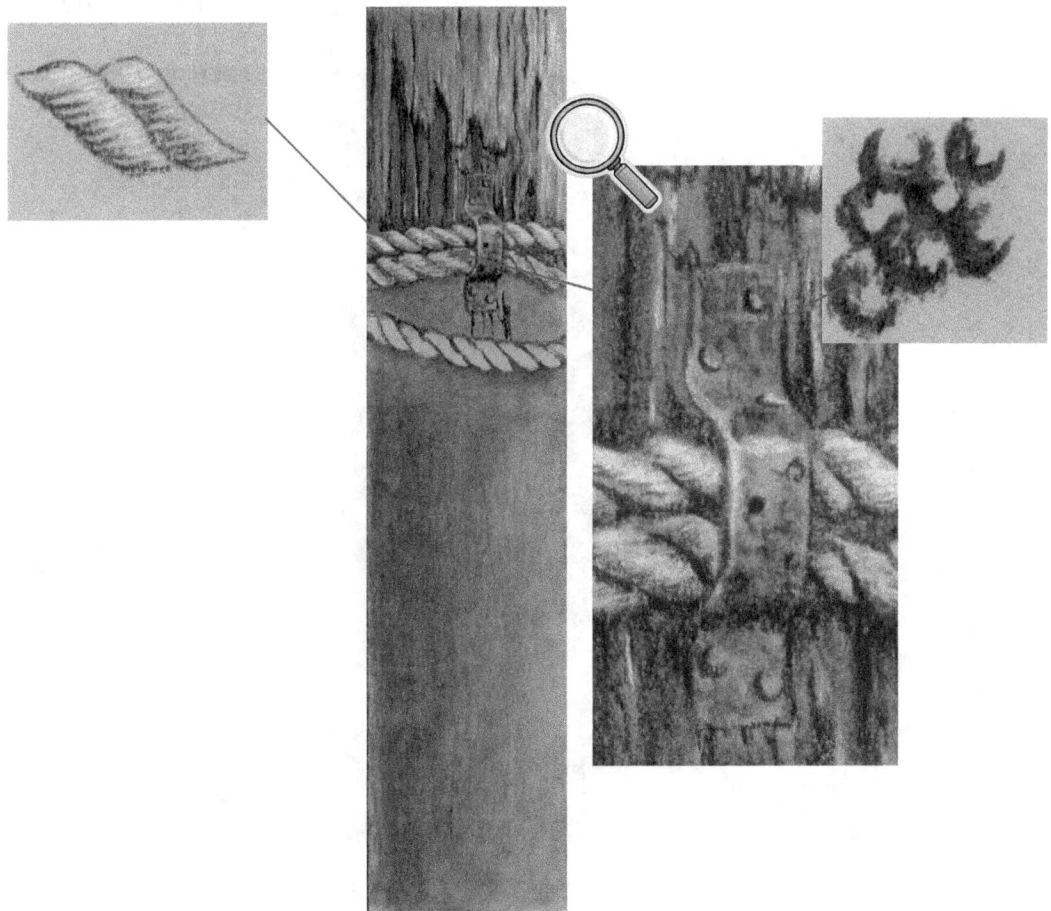

Fig. 53.

www.DrawPJ.com

Step Four: Complete the area between the ropes

1. Using a sharp *2B charcoal pencil* continue to draw the jagged lines of the shadow shapes and crevices in the wood texture. Work in the small section between the second and third ropes. Constantly refer to the photograph (see Fig. 50a) to seek out the largest and darkest shadow areas first. Apply the same techniques you just used to draw the top section (see Fig. 54.)
2. Add finer hatching lines to create more texture then complete this area by adding a touch of white Conté to highlight some areas of the wood.
3. Complete the texture on the third (bottom) rope (see Fig. 54.)

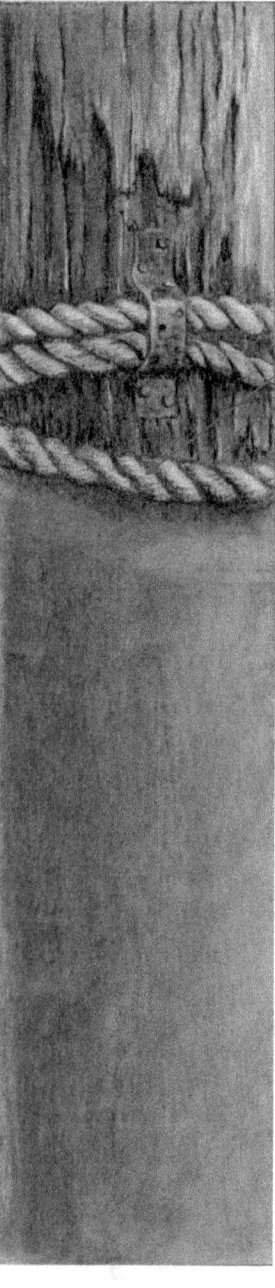

Continue to travel down the post completing the entire top section of the drawing including the third rope.

Fig. 54.

Step Five: Continue to make your way down the post

1. To make it easier to complete the large section beneath the ropes, divide the section in half vertically. Measure half-way along the bottom and top of the rectangle. Only rule this centre guideline up to the bottom edge of the rope as you have already completed the upper section and we do not wish to disturb this area. Rule a vertical line through the centre of the area on your photograph (see Fig. 50a) as well as on your drawing like you can see here (see Fig. 55.)
2. Mark half-way and quarter way marks along the vertical sides of the rectangle. Use these lines as guides to help you place the largest and darkest shapes using your 2B charcoal pencil. Once you have placed the darkest shapes it is easier to place the smaller shapes. Work in just the left half first and gradually make your way across to the right.

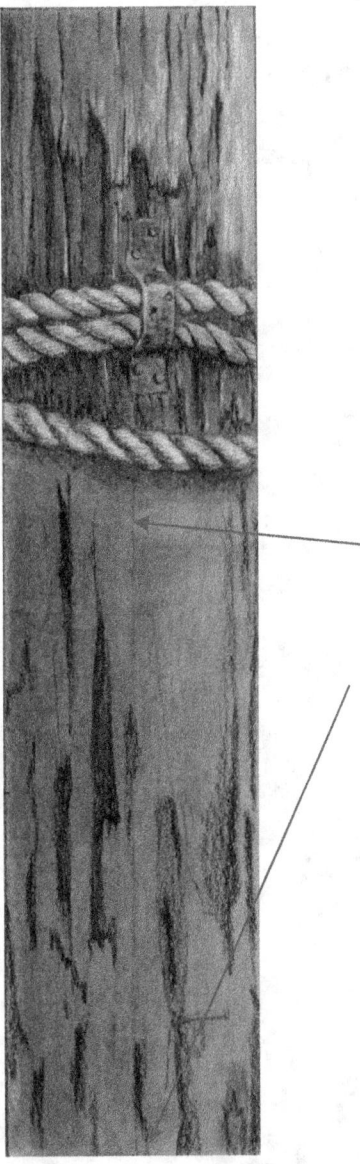

Rule a centre vertical line through the bottom area to help you with the placement of the largest dark shaped areas. In drawing it often helps to halve a larger area and draw in just one half of the area at a time

Fig. 55.

Step Six: Complete the wood grain by using your putty eraser to expose the paper ready to add white Conté

1. After you have drawn the major dark shapes, putty out the lighter areas then apply white Conté for your final highlights (see Fig. 56a.)
2. Once you have done that your drawing is complete (see Fig. 56b.)

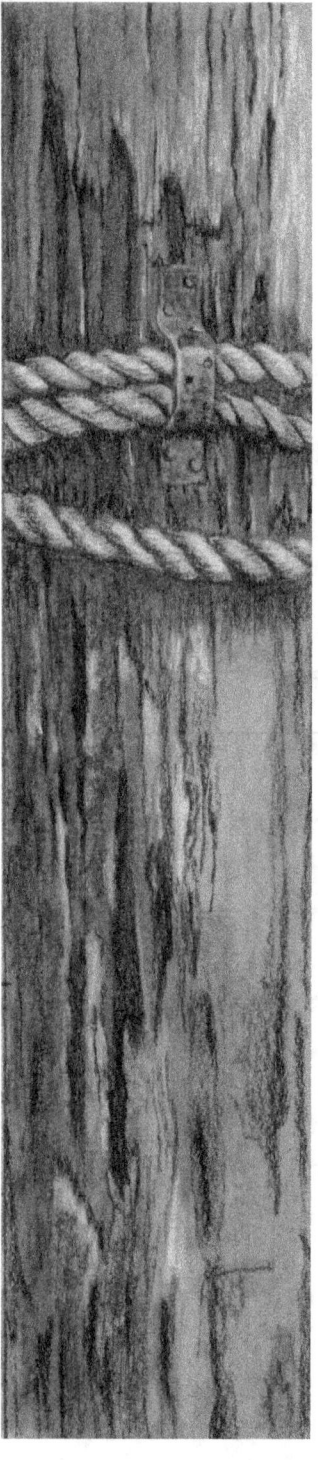
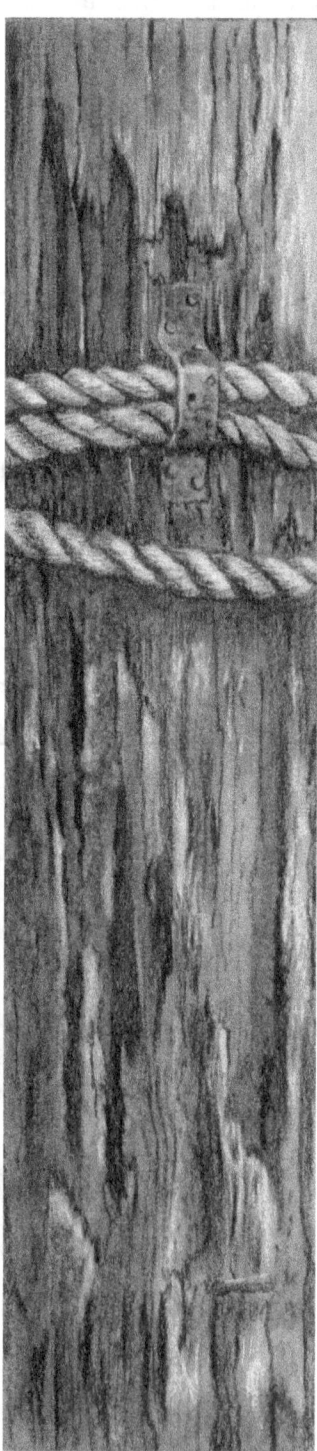

Fig. 56a.   Fig. 56b.

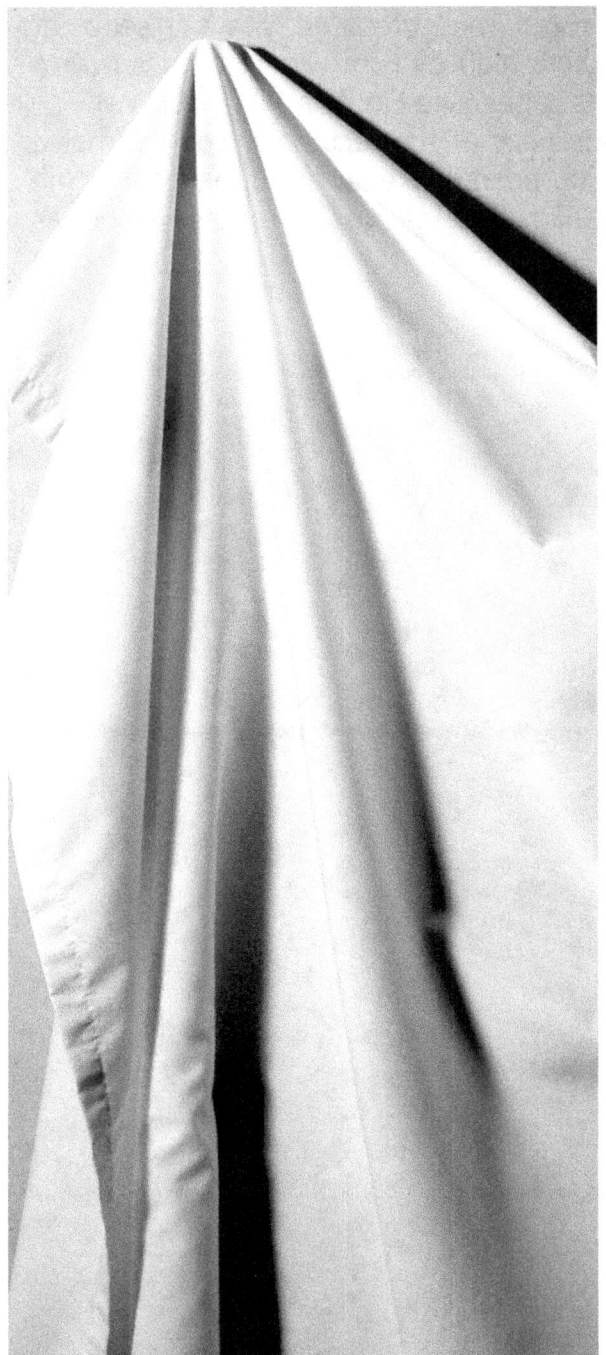

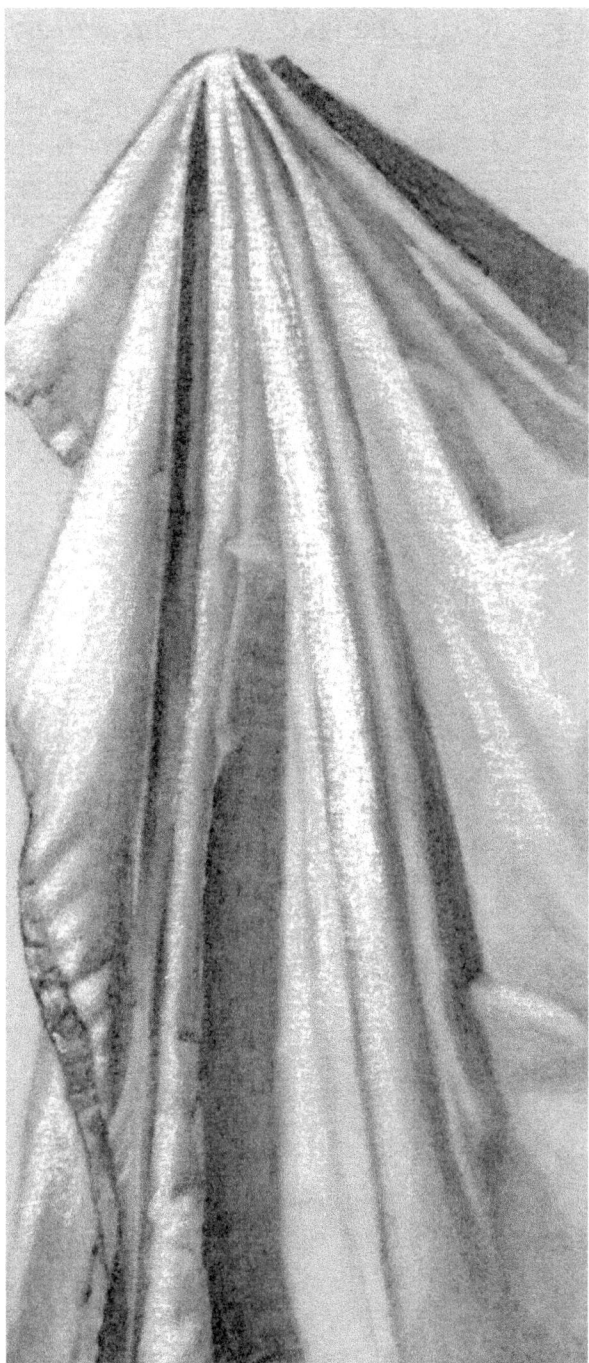

Fig. 57a. Photograph of 'Drapery'   Fig. 57b. Drawing of 'Drapery'

Step One: Draw the outline of the drapery

1. Use the tip of your **thin willow charcoal stick** prepared with a chisel point and your ruler to draw a rectangle 18cm high by 8cm wide on the **smooth side** of a sheet of pale grey Mi-Teintes paper (see Fig. 58a.)
2. Mark half and quarter way on all four sides of the rectangle. You can halve these areas again as many times as you need. Make sure you mark the same halving lines on the photograph (see Fig. 57a) as well. Use these marks as guidelines to compare the position of each line to.

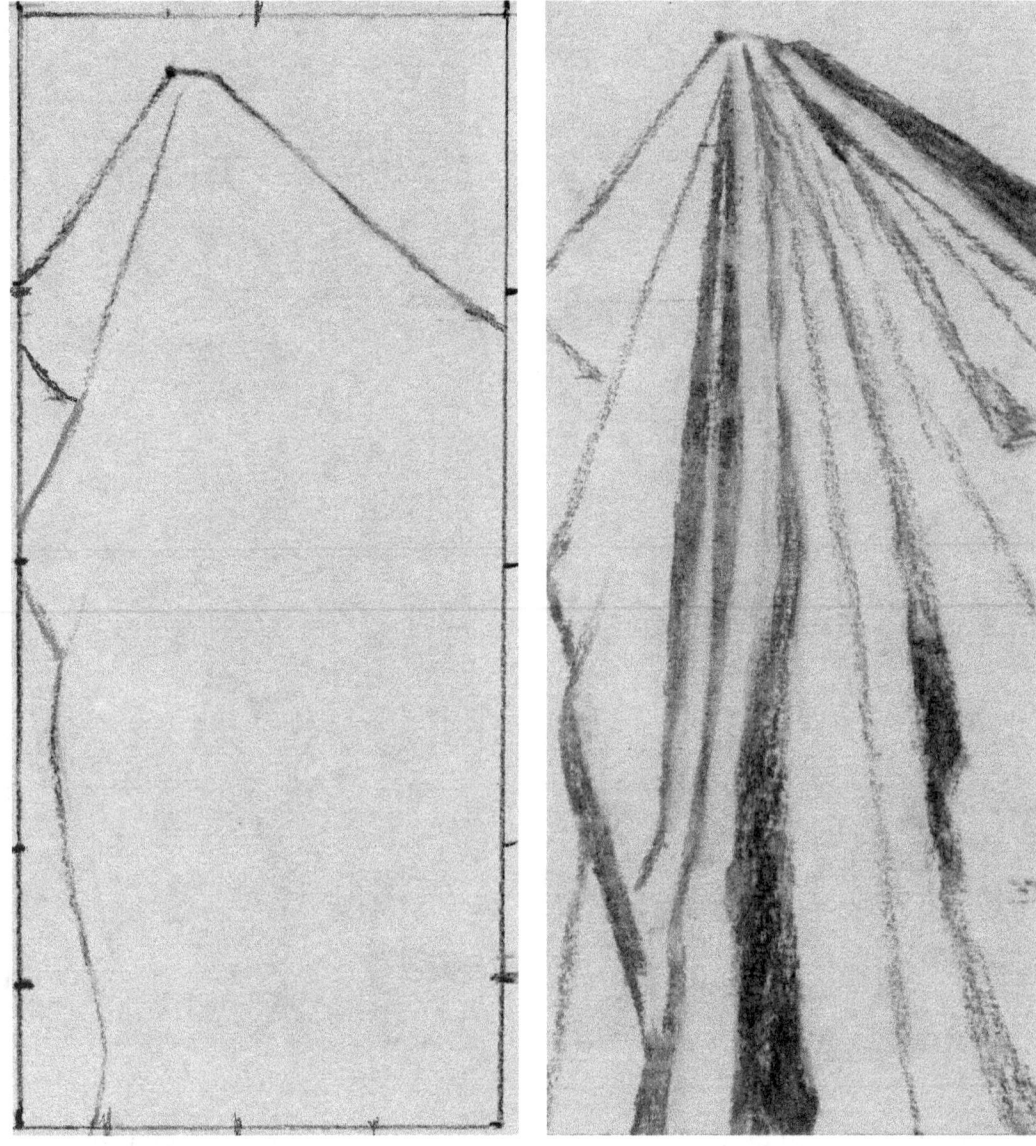

Fig. 58a.   Fig. 58b.

3. Copy the line drawing around the outside of the drape. Use the photograph to measure from and the drawing as a guide to indicate what shapes to draw (see Figs. 57a and 58a.) You can draw the shapes accurately by using your ruler to measure the distance of the angles from the top or sides of the rectangle, or work more loosely and just compare to the halfway marks. You could begin by measuring how far down from the top the very beginning of the drape is, then how far in the drape begins from the left side. Make small dashes to mark the positions of each part of the drape then draw the simple outline as shown in the example (see Fig. 58a.)
4. Once you have completed the outline of the drape, use your willow charcoal stick to shade in all the major angles of the drape. Refer to the original photograph as a guide and the drawing as an indicator of the types of shapes you need to draw (see Fig. 58b.)

Step Two: Blend the shadow shapes using your paper stump

1. Blend in all of the lines and angles as well as the shadow shapes with your paper stump by following the direction of the fold (see Fig. 59.)
2. Apply more willow charcoal to the darker shadow areas (see Fig. 59.)

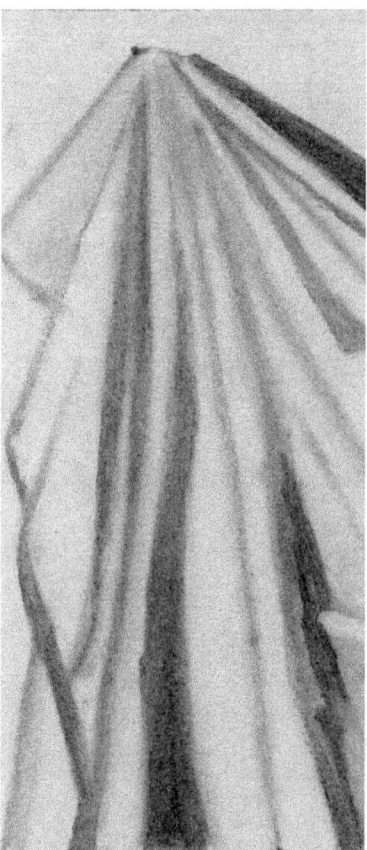

Fig. 59.

www.DrawPJ.com

Step Three: Refine the shadow shapes using your willow charcoal

1. Use the tip of your willow charcoal stick prepared to a chisel point to begin refining the shapes of the shadows including the tiny details along the edges of the drape (see Fig. 60.) In the photograph (see Fig. 57a) it doesn't show the delicate folds along the left side so we have to use our artistic licence to 'make up the drawing in that area.'

2. We do not always draw everything we see in the photograph, we often have to provide more information in our drawing, or sometimes less depending on what we feel is important to the successful depiction of the image. Use the drawing provided this time for your main guide (see Fig. 57b.)

Draw the fine details and refine the shadow shapes using your willow charcoal.

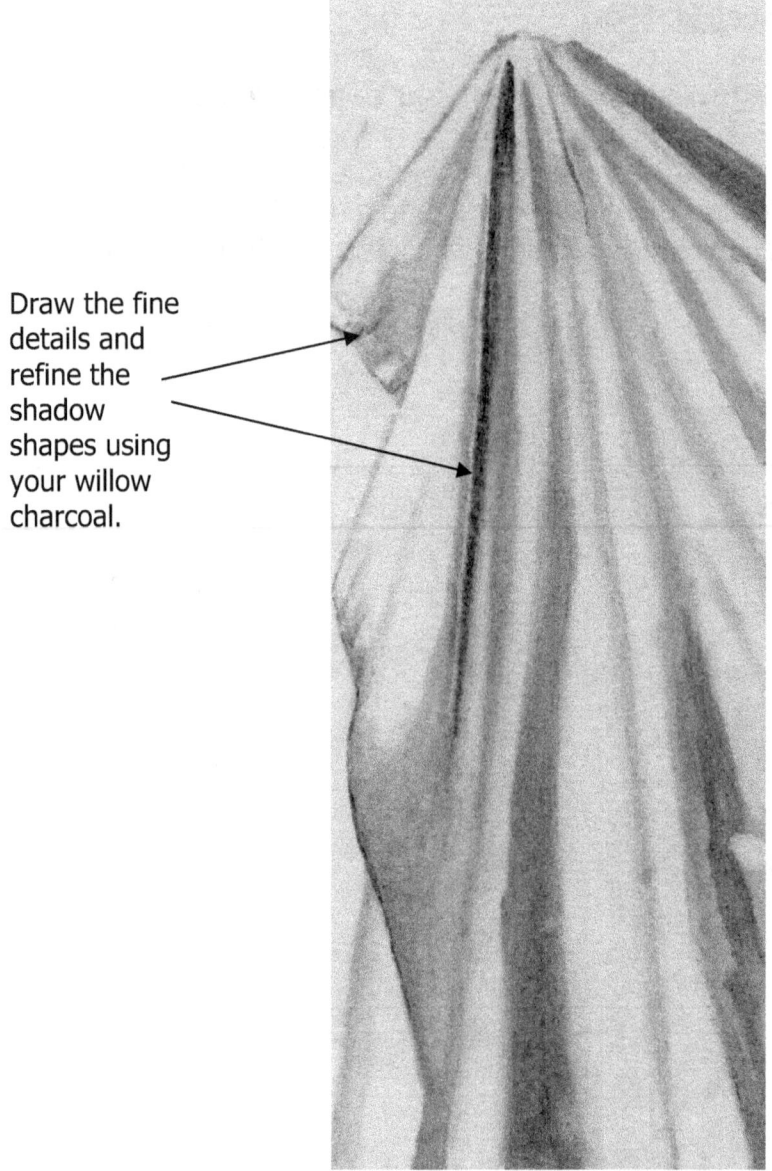

Fig. 60.

Step Four: Begin to draw the highlights using your putty eraser

Use your putty eraser and stump to draw the shapes of the small details and refine the highlight areas (see insert Fig. 61.)

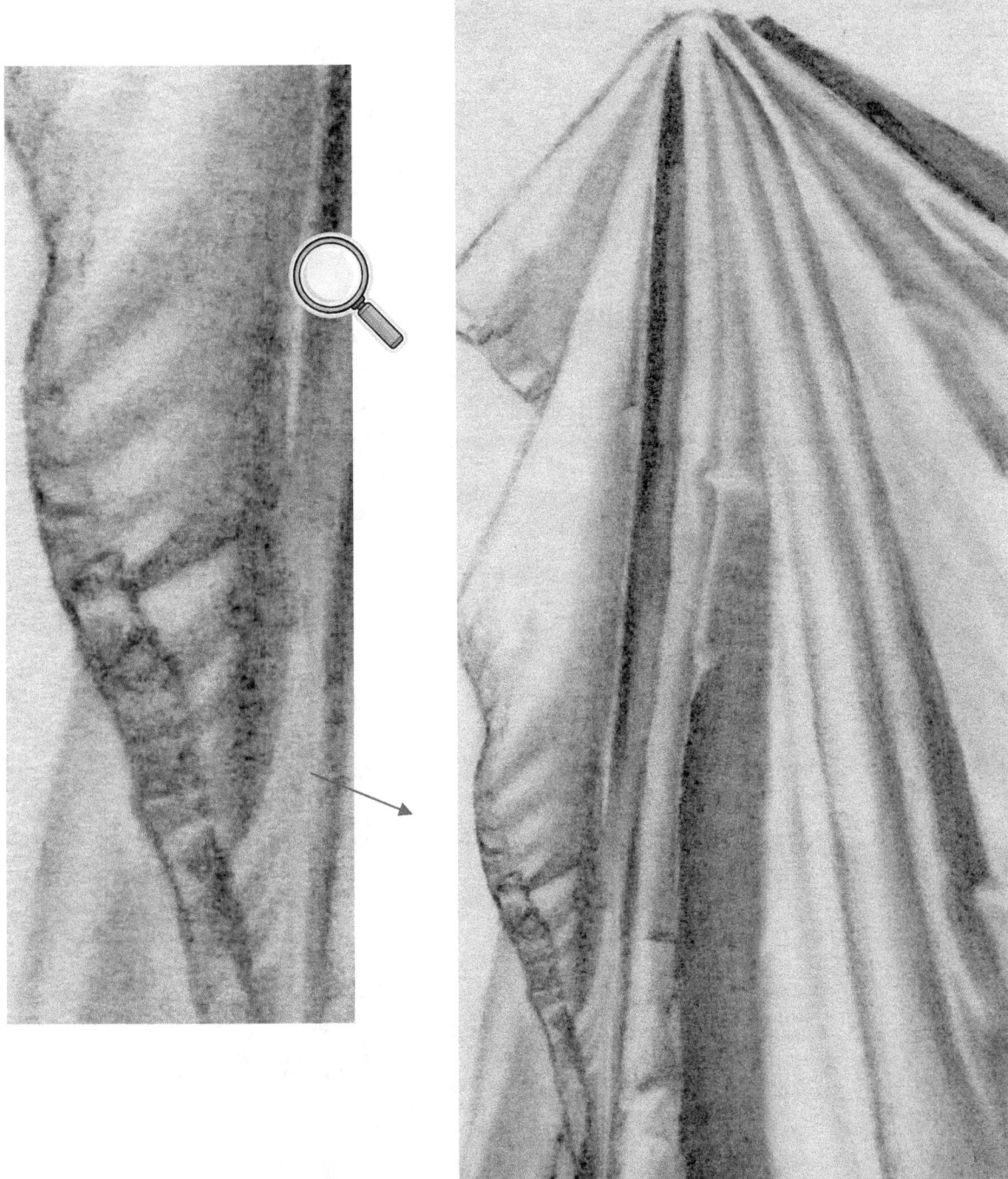

Fig. 61.

www.DrawPJ.com

Step Five: Add white Conté as a finishing touch to the highlights

1. Use your white Conté prepared to a chisel point to add the shapes of the lightest highlights. Include some tiny details along the edges of the drape (see Figs. 62.) Use the larger surface of the Conté to shade the larger highlight areas.
2. Once you have finalised this step, you drawing is complete.

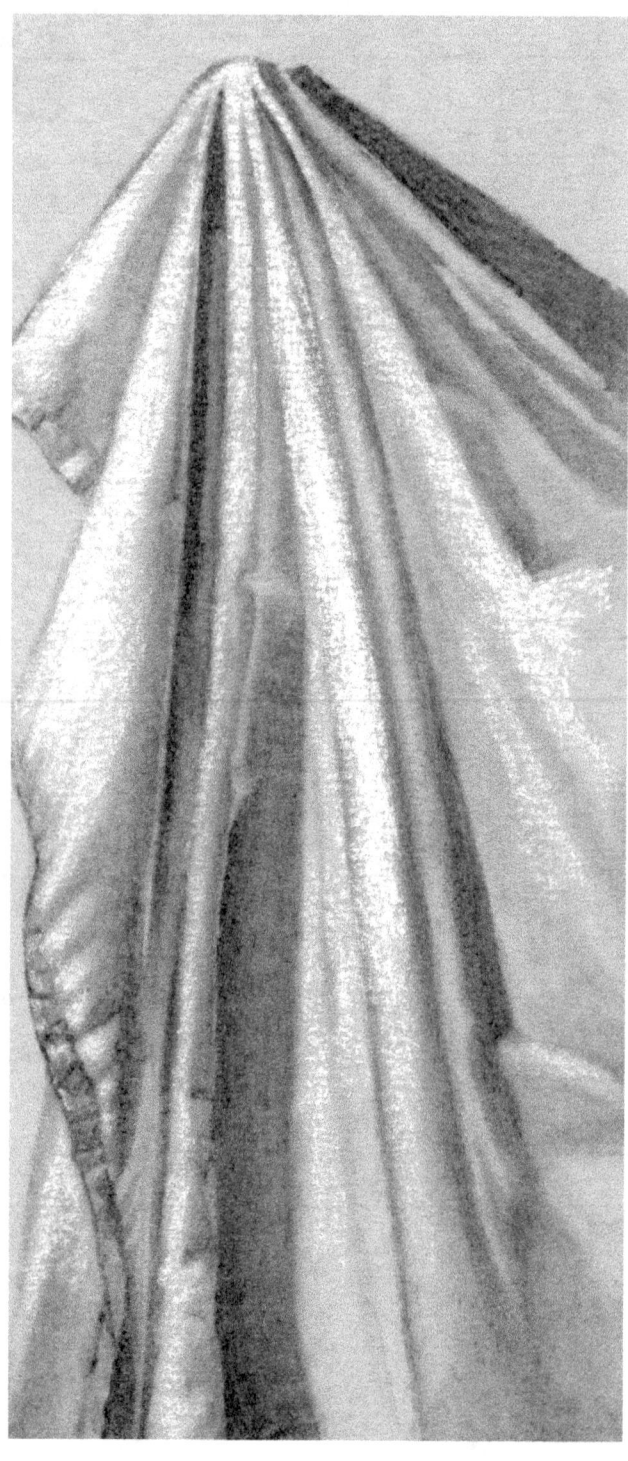

Fig. 62.

Summary for week three

The exercises this week will give you the opportunity to further instil the knowledge you learned in the previous weeks of the course notes. Charcoal is an amazing medium and once mastered you can easily achieve a whole array of textures through creative application of the techniques you have now learned.

If you didn't have the opportunity to draw any of the hairstyles last week, I highly recommend that you consider doing that for your exercise this week. The hairstyles are very important for your final project which begins next week.

Enjoy the process and remember that learning to draw requires practice. Practice as much as you can, and the charcoal techniques will all just fall into place naturally. Charcoal works best if you are relaxed. The best way to be relaxed is to smile while you work. Smiling relaxes your entire upper torso. Try to involve your full body when you work by squirming, bending, moving as you draw.

Remember to 'Just show up at your table' and the rest will take care of itself! Have a fun week.

www.DrawPJ.com

Weeks Four and Five

Introduction to weeks four and five

Last week you were again given the opportunity to practice a variety of different charcoal techniques in the step-by-step drawings of three different objects. Everything you have learned so far in this course was to prepare you for your project which is a portrait drawing. There are no more weekly courses to study as you are now entering the project stage of the course (week four and five.) You have two weeks to create your final drawing 'A completed Portrait.' You may choose to take week four to gather your reference photographs if you choose to create a portrait of either yourself or someone you know.

Please do not use copyright protected images from magazines and other artists work. Do your best to create your own photograph (or you are very welcome to use the photograph provided.) If you are creating your own photograph, make sure that the sitter's head is in the position suggested in your notes this week. The notes are designed to help you create a portrait in the front on position which is a great place to start with portraiture.

It is traditional art practice to learn how to draw portraits of people (most often from life as well as photographs) and there is a very good reason for this. Studying portraiture provides you with a wonderful opportunity to explore many complex shapes and forms that provide a great challenge and excellent training ground for art students.

This week, you will choose to either create a 'Self Portrait' a portrait of a friend (using a photograph taken after applying the suggestions provided shortly in the course this week) or draw the portrait of a woman provided here for you. If you are drawing yourself and the features in your photo are not clear enough for you to draw small details from, look at yourself in a mirror. Just keep in mind that the image you see in the mirror will appear opposite to the image in the photograph. This is not always obvious, but you can notice it when drawing hair in particular. Your drawing is to be created using Charcoal with white Conté on grey Mi-Teintes paper.

To help you draw your portrait, you have been provided with a step-by-step process which demonstrates the procedure you can use along with your ***own photograph*** to create your drawing. If you have not been able to take a photograph of yourself or someone you know, you are welcome to use the photograph provided here (see Fig. 1) along with the instructions provided. The Portrait drawn here was created using charcoal and white Conté on grey Mi-Teintes paper is titled, 'Just Me' (see Fig.2.) This project is broken down into small steps and stages so that you can more easily achieve the end result. Take your time to do your best work and enjoy the process.

Important: please read your notes right through to the Final Words section before beginning your project.

Position of features on an adult face

Take a look at the face shape provided below to notice the position of the features on an average adult Caucasian head. This is only a guide, naturally people vary slightly from these basic positions, but most adult features are very close to these standards. Different races of people have similar but slightly different positions for features, and you can do some research to see how your particular race differs to the person here. Use the position of features that suits you as an individual after using these as a starting point.

1. The eye-line is halfway down the face. You have just measured the position of the eye-line relative to your face (see number 1.)

2. The eyes are positioned along the eye-line (see number 2.) Most adult faces measure approximately five eyes wide with one eye width separating the two eyes and one on either side of the face between the eye and the widest part of the head. Please note, it is often hard to see the full width of your head because it is covered in hair. You can gently press the side of your skull to feel for the maximum width if you are unable to visualise where that is.

   Sometimes there might be a smaller gap between the two eyes, and occasionally there are people with heads not quite as wide on either side of the eyes. These people usually have a long narrow face. You could divide this eye-line into five equal sections by using your pencil, but in this case, you can save time by simply dividing it with your ruler into 3cm intervals. Make sure you place a 3 cm width centred across the middle vertical line (central axis) so that the eyes are centred and one eye-width apart. Draw some round dark dots to indicate the pupils and make sure they are in the centre of each eye.

3. The tip of the nose is not quite one-half but more than one-third of the distance between the eye-line and bottom of the chin (see number 3.) You can make a mark at half-way between the eye-line and the chin on your drawing then measure the position of your nose (see number 7.) Keep your face straight on whenever measuring. Use the sighting method and line your pencil up with the tip in line with your eye-line and your thumb in line with the base of your chin.

   Look to see where half-way is between this distance then visually compare how close your nose is to the half-way distance on your face. Is it on the half-way or above? Is it on the one-third way mark or below that? Remember where it is compared to these measurements then draw a small line on the vertical axis.

4. The middle of the lip (the gap between the lips) can be found about one third of the distance between the tip of the nose and the chin (see number 4.) Again compare this standard measurement to your own measurement and place a small dash on the vertical line to indicate its position.

5. If you draw a vertical line straight down from the inside corner of your eye, you will find the outside tip of your nostril (see number 5.) Your nose might be different these are standard measurements and do not apply to everyone so adjust your head accordingly. You can draw some little curved shapes to indicate nostrils.

6. The top of the ear is in line with somewhere between the area below your eyebrow and above your open eye-lid. Make a mark to indicate where your ear is (see number 6.)

7. The bottom of the ear is in line with somewhere between the area of skin between the top of the lip and the very lowest part of your nose (see number 7.) Make a mark to indicate where yours is and draw a symbol for an ear as is done here.

8. The corners of the mouth when slightly smiling are directly in line with the middle of the eye if you draw a vertical line down from there.

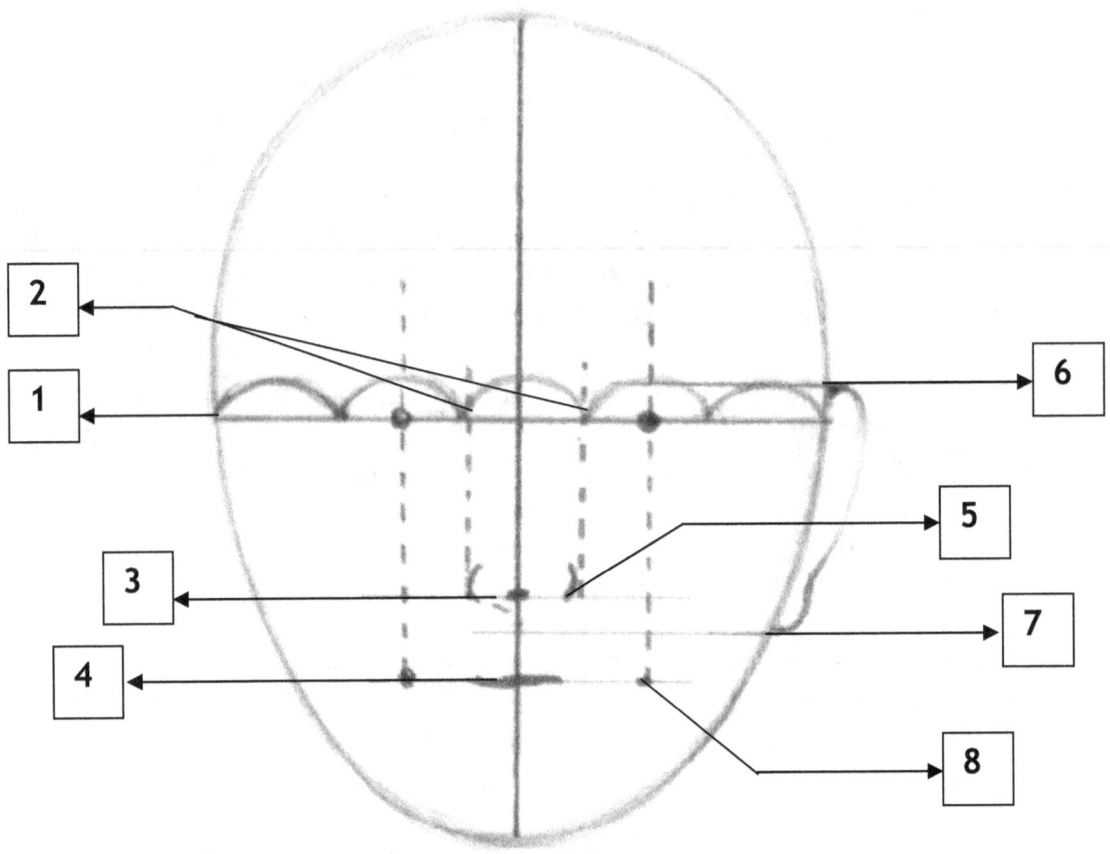

Placement of the features on a Caucasian human adult face

Take a photograph for your final portraiture project

Your task is to take a good clear photograph either of yourself (preferred) or of a friend to use as a reference source to produce your charcoal portrait drawing from. Alternatively you can use the photograph in these notes (see Fig. 1) to create your final portrait from. Your drawing will be an expressive interpretation based upon a likeness to the subject (see Figs. 1 and 2.) If you choose to take a photograph of yourself you can either set the timer on your camera to allow you time to sit down in position. Better still, get someone else to press the button for you.

Make sure you either use a tripod or rest your camera on a solid surface at the correct height to take your photograph as blurred images are difficult to work from. It isn't wise to trust the human hand to hold the camera in case you move the camera accidently which can easily produce a blurred image. It is different of course if you are an experienced professional photographer. This photograph will need to be changed to grey-scale (using a photo-editing software program such as Photoshop Elements) to enable you to more easily compare tonal values.

Here are some important things to consider in order to take a successful photograph to use as a reference for your final project;

1. Set up the scene with a plain white background such as a wall in your home or a hanging-sheet so that there are no distractions in the background. There is an emphasis on just the face and mainly and a little bit on the shoulders for this photograph.

2. Place a single bright light source such as a strong lamp (not a fluorescent bulb as these tend to flatten out the shadows making it harder to see the image) to the left or right and at least a couple of meters out in front of the seat where you will be sitting.

3. Take a test photo to make sure that your camera is in line with your face ie: so that your head is included in the main area of the photograph.

4. Take two photos of the exact same pose as follows;

    ➤ The first one should include your face, hair, neck and the start of your shoulders. Make sure you include the very top and sides of your hair. Only leave a little bit of space around the image when you are taking your photo to ensure it is as close as you can be without cropping sections off.
    ➤ The second photo is to be an even closer image of your forehead to chin. This one is for a close up of your eyes, nose and mouth. Hold your pose extremely still so that the photos are the same.

5. Position your head carefully so that we can use the division of eyes half-way down the head etc. This means that you need to make sure your face is front on to the camera. You can tilt it to either side or even have it looking straight on (easier) but don't tilt it up, down or turn around to a three-quarter view etc. Use a delicate 'traditional portrait smile of no teeth.' I call this pose the 'Mona Lisa plus' smile, in other words have that almost non-smile that the famous painting by Leonardo Da Vinci's Mona Lisa has, **_with just a touch more of a smile_**. If you smile too much, your entire face will change the guidelines for you. Also, we will be concentrating on drawing the complex shapes and lines that form the area where the two lips meet.

6. Do not shake or move the camera whatsoever while you are pressing the button. Take at least ten or twenty photographs and then choose the best one – with matching close-up to use as your favourite.

7. Once you have taken your photographs alter the images to grey scale and enhance it using photo-editing software by gently increasing contrast so that it is clear for you to see the shadows and highlights without too much dramatic tonal difference. Take your time with this photograph as it is crucial to the success of your portrait.

Tip: If you have chosen to draw from the photograph provided at Fig. 1 you may choose to print the image out on high quality photographic printing paper for a more clear image.

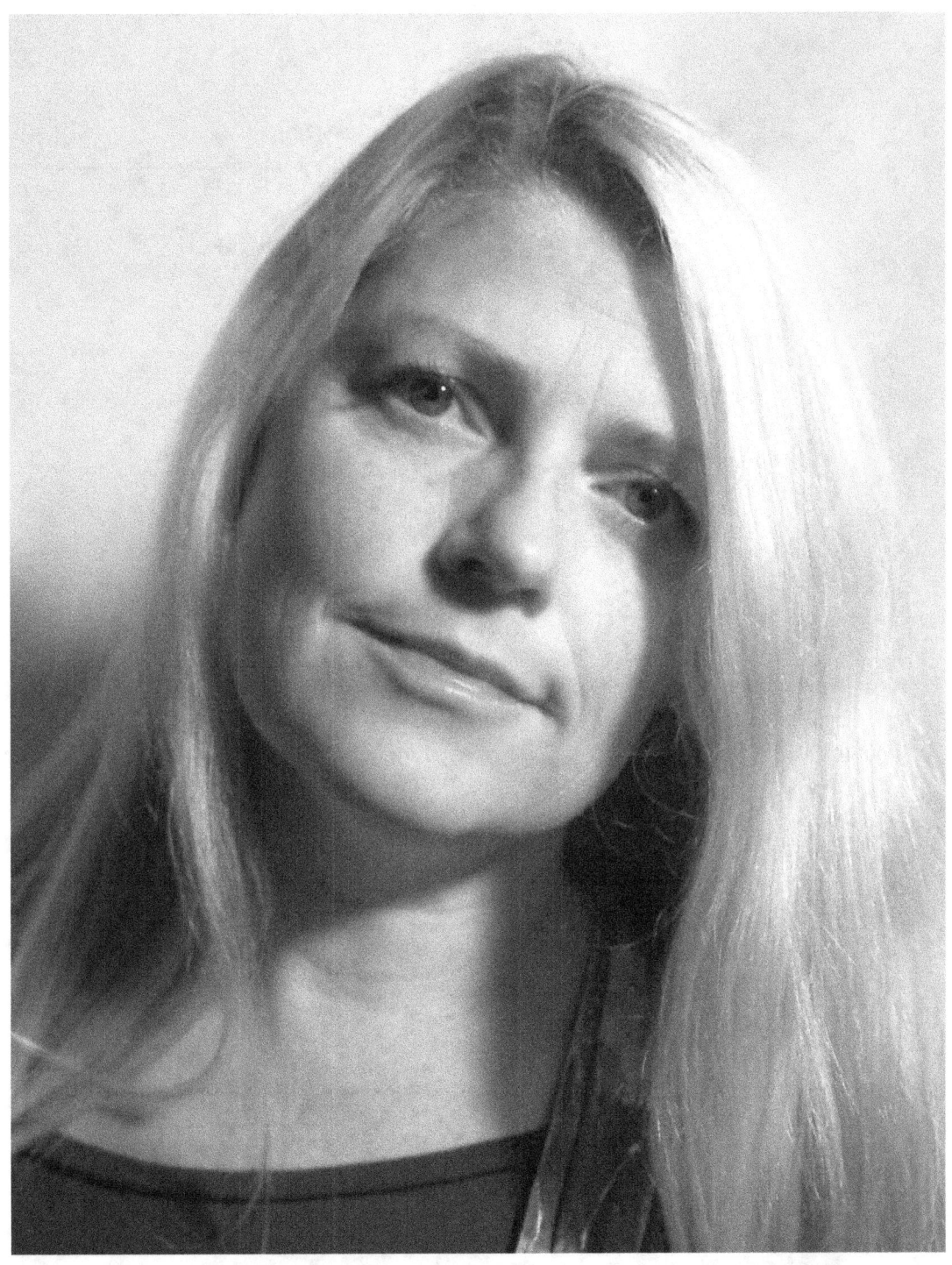

Fig. 1. Photograph of 'Just Me'

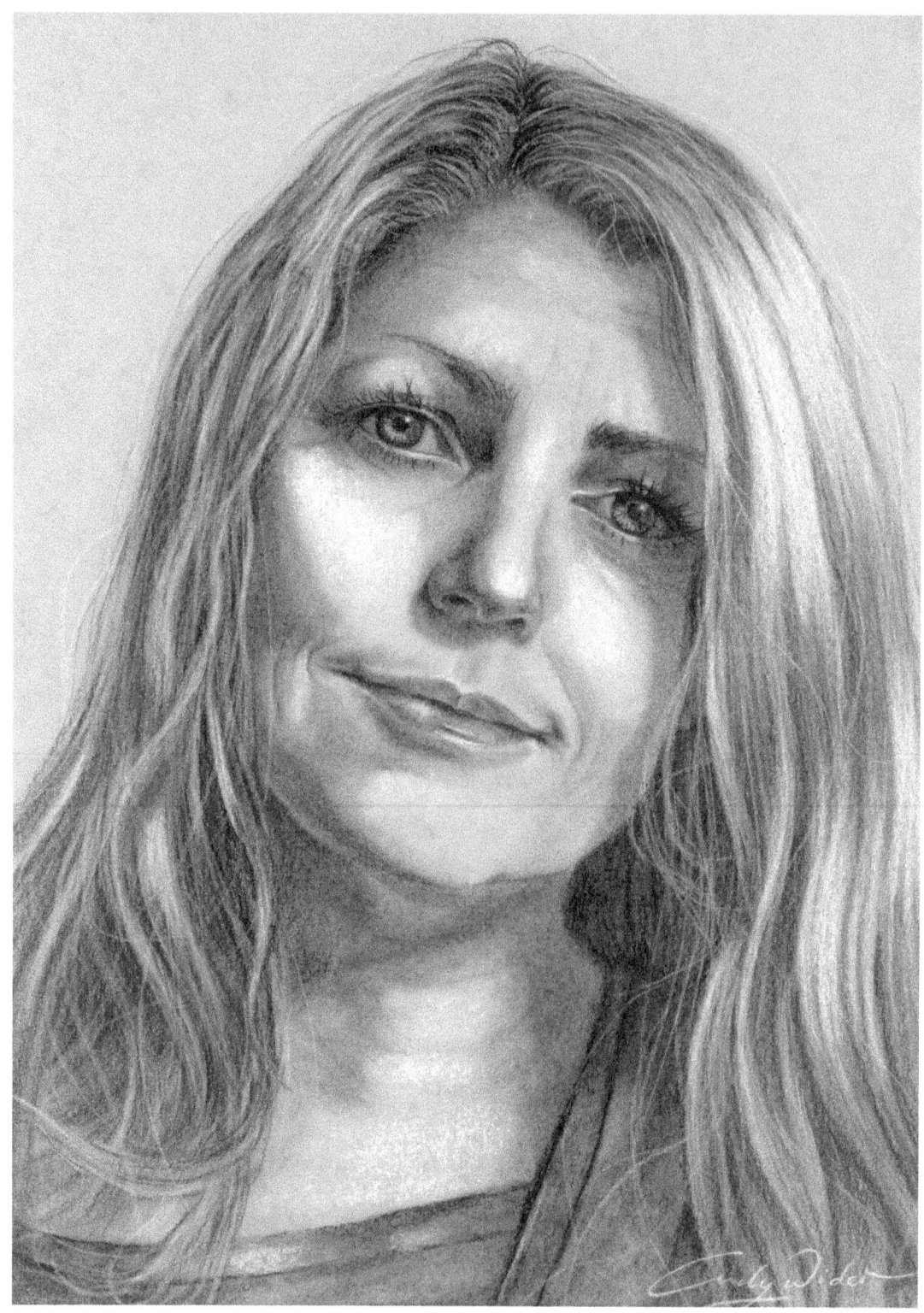

Fig. 2. Final Charcoal and white Conté drawing of 'Just Me'

Final project step-by-step portrait example: 'Just Me'

This section provides you with a step-by-step example of how you can approach drawing your own portrait in charcoal with white conte on grey mi-teintes paper.

You may have chosen to draw yourself, or someone you know, or you are welcome to use this photograph to draw from. If you have chosen to take your own photograph (recommended for the best experience of this project) you can use the same steps that are demonstrated here but apply the information to your own photograph. In some sections you will also be asked to refer back to your *week two* notes on how to draw hair.

Step One: Mark in the initial guidelines

1. First of all print out your photograph on high quality printing paper to make sure your image is beautiful and clear. Then place a sheet of clear acetate or a plastic sleeve over the photograph of 'Just Me' (see Fig. 1) and tape it in three places across the top only. This is so that you can lift the sheet up and down to see the photograph more clearly if needed. You will be drawing on this clear acetate sheet first (using a permanent marker pen) so that you can discover and measure the guidelines you see demonstrated here (see Fig. 3.)

2. Use your ruler and permanent marker to rule the following guidelines onto the clear sheet over the top of your photograph. Notice there is a central axis drawn on a diagonal, down the middle of the face here (see Fig. 3.) Along this line there are other lines **drawn at a right angle to this centre line** which indicate the eye-line, tip of the nose and middle lip line. Even though the head is tilted and therefore the central axis is tilted (on a diagonal), these lines remain at a right angle to the central axis. When the head is front on and not tilted, the central axis is draw exactly vertical and the nose, middle lip and eye line are still at a right angle. This is the secret to avoiding skewed features; keep the features parallel to one another and at a right angle to the central vertical line.

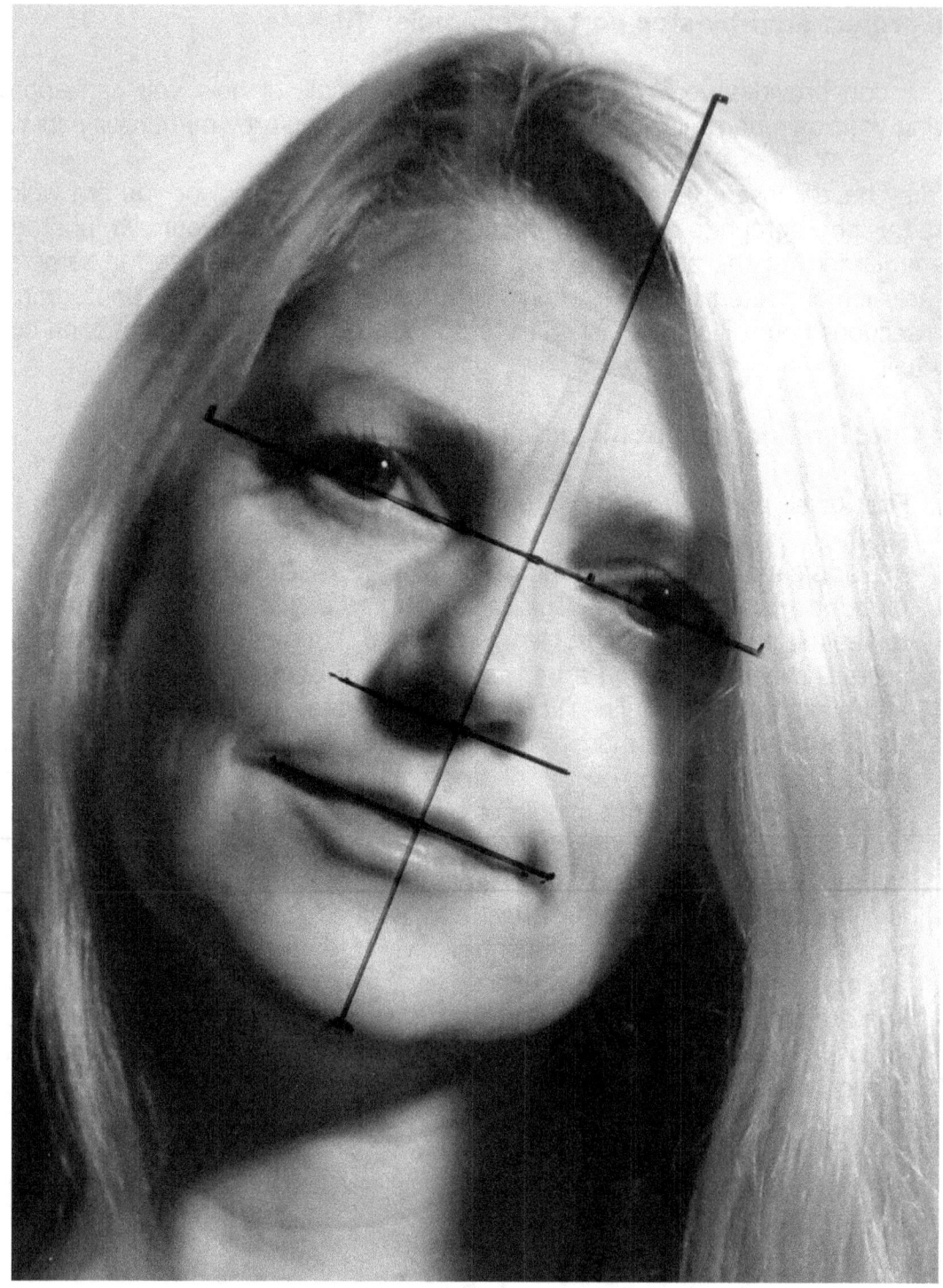

Fig. 3. Initial guide lines drawn onto a clear sheet covering the photograph

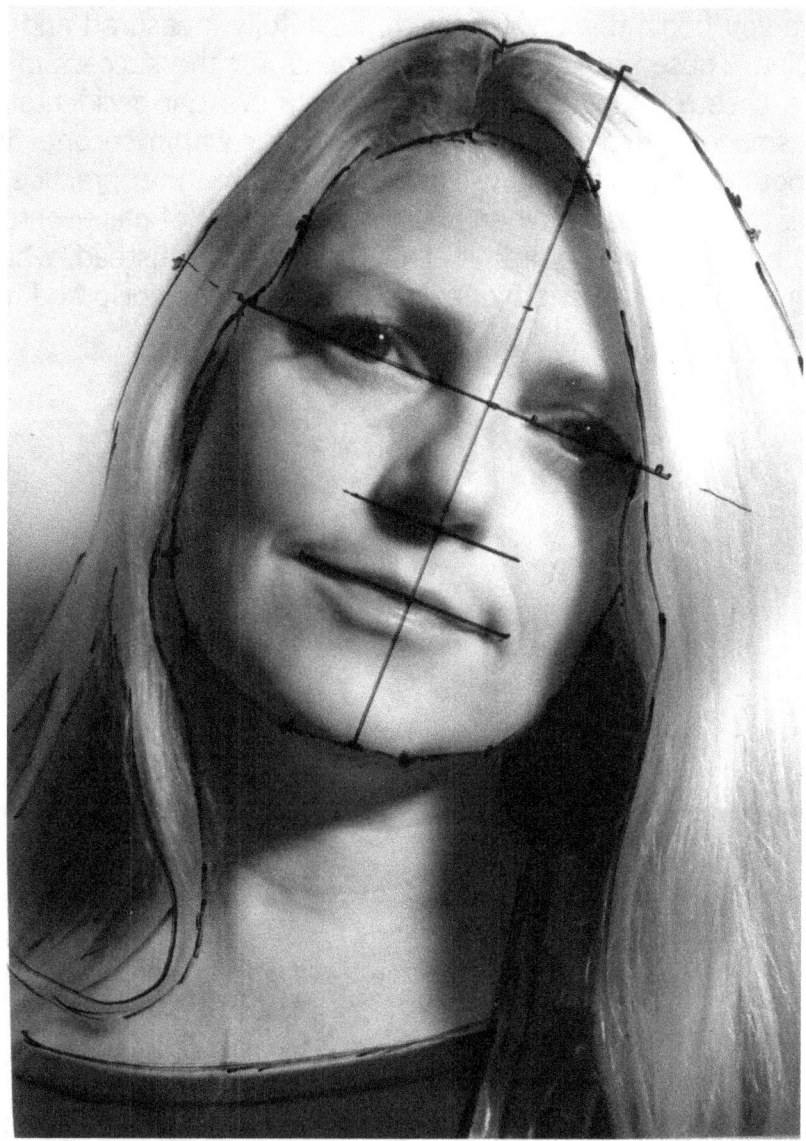

Fig. 4a. Basic Outlines of the face and hair drawn onto a clear sheet

Step Two: Continue to draw the basic outline of the face and hair

1. Still drawing on the acetate sheet placed over the photograph, continue to place the lines or curves for the hair, face and shirt that you see here in black lines (Fig. 4a.) Note that these are mostly just angles and not the final curves you see in the photograph.

2. Once you have completed the angles for the hair and face, it is time to **begin drawing this same image onto the smooth side of your grey Mi-Teintes paper**. Use the tip of your **willow charcoal prepared with a chisel point** and your ruler to accurately measure and **softly** draw these initial guidelines (see Fig. 4b.) Rule and measure the central axis and guide lines first then measure as many places as you like. Don't use your charcoal pencil it won't erase properly and please press softly with your willow stick.

Tip: Make sure you begin this drawing with a carefully measured and drawn central axis and eye-line. These are crucial measurements for the success of your portrait. Always place a sheet of paper under your hand to prevent accidentally erasing the image due to smudging. Your drawing can disappear within seconds if you are not careful. All is not lost however, you will get a chance to further practice your valuable drawing skills if this is the case. When you place the sheet of paper onto your work to protect it, also be careful not to drag it across the surface. Instead, when moving the sheet, gently lift it off the surface by peeling it back, picking it up and moving it.

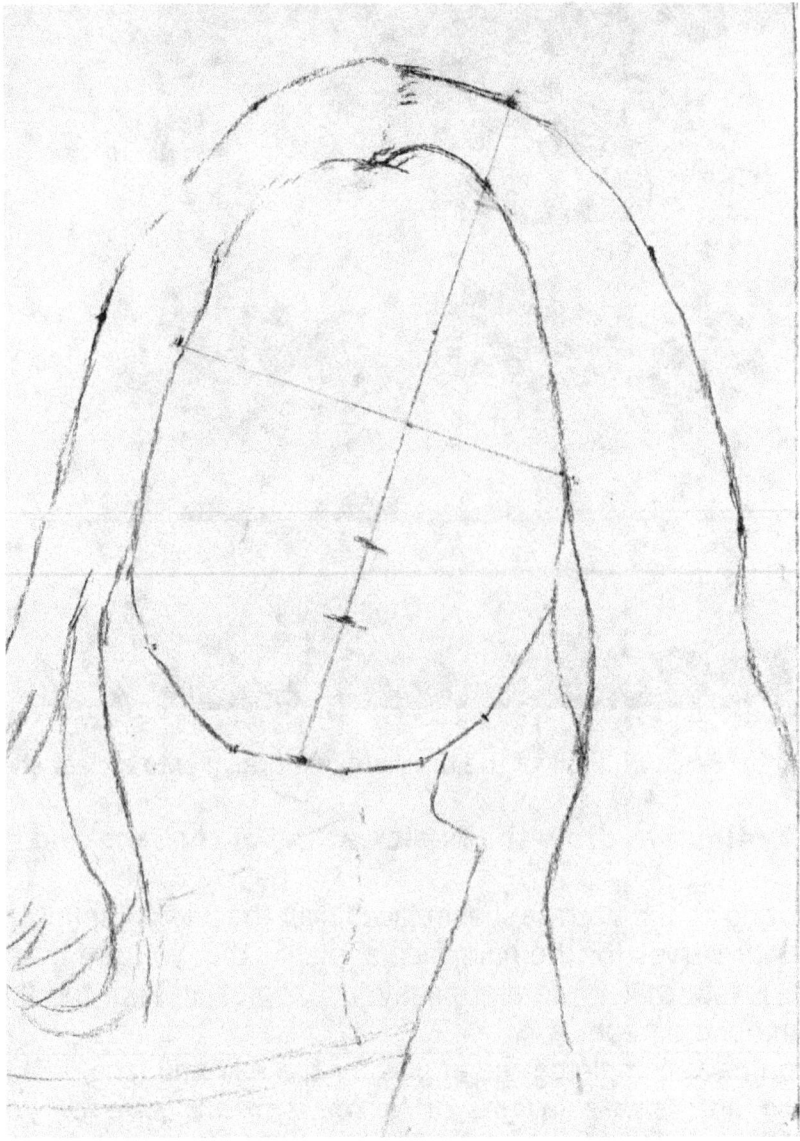

Fig. 4b. Basic Outlines of the face and hair drawn onto Mi-Teintes paper

www.DrawPJ.com

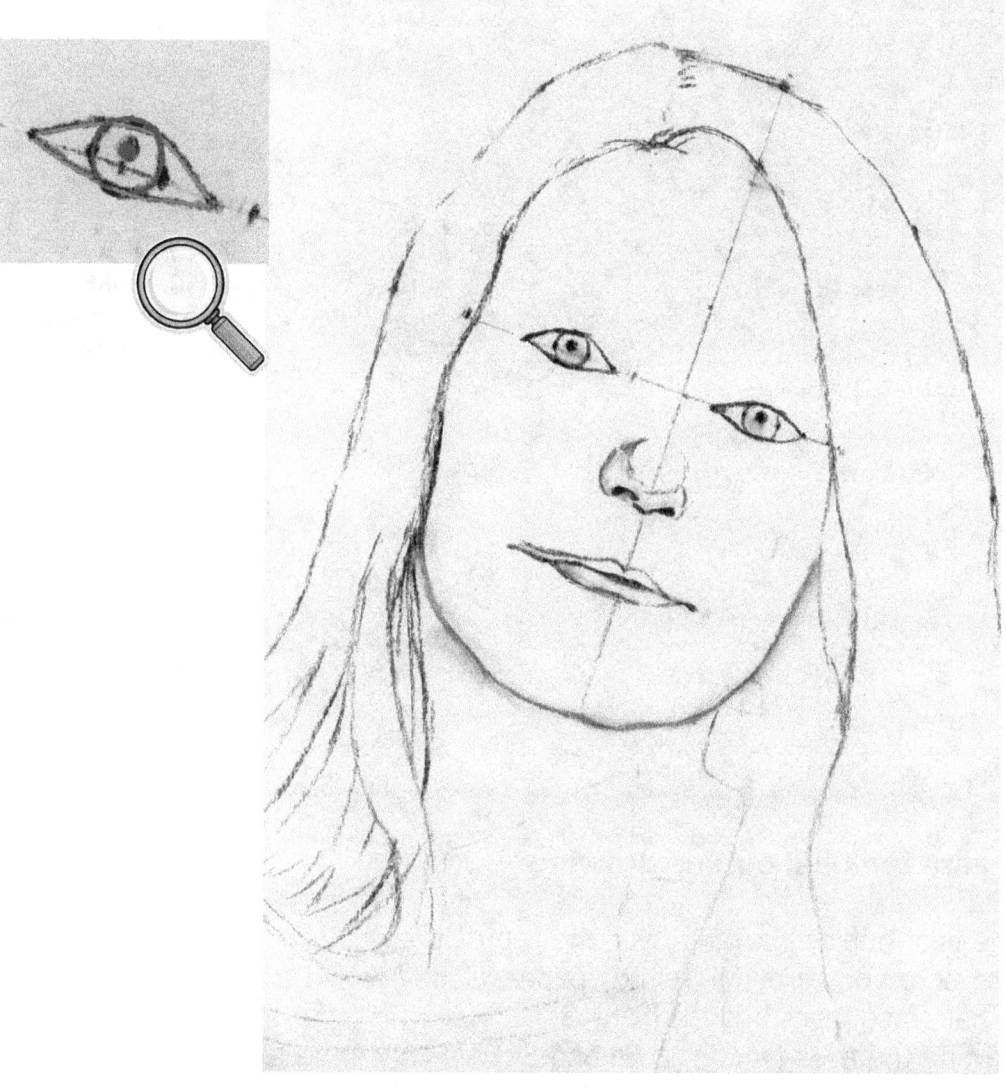

Fig. 5a. Final outline drawing of the face

Tip on how to draw eyes:
1. First of all draw a cross 3cm x 3cm (see Fig. 5b)
2. Then draw a circle around the cross (see Fig. 5c.)
3. Then draw two smaller circles within this circle (see Fig. 5d.)
4. The draw the outline of any shadow and highlight shapes (see Fig. 5e.)

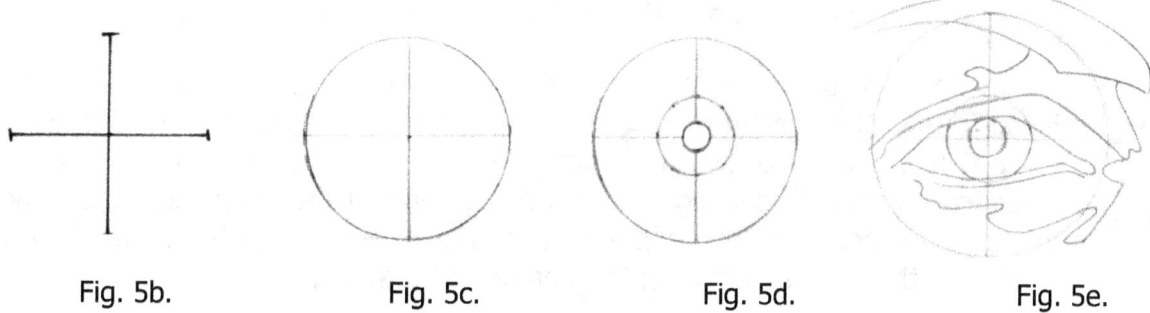

Fig. 5b.   Fig. 5c.   Fig. 5d.   Fig. 5e.

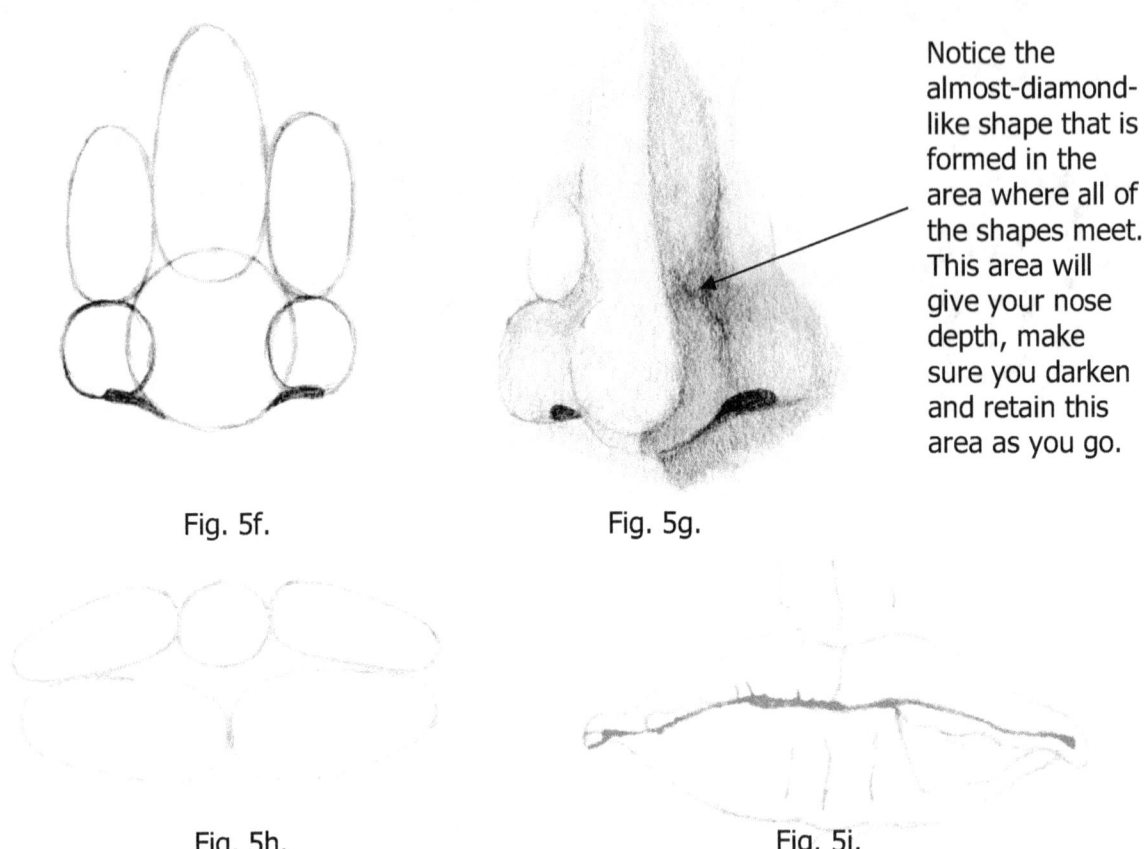

Notice the almost-diamond-like shape that is formed in the area where all of the shapes meet. This area will give your nose depth, make sure you darken and retain this area as you go.

Fig. 5f.

Fig. 5g.

Fig. 5h.

Fig. 5i.

Step Three: Create the final outline drawing

1. Create the final outline drawing over the top of the guidelines that you have just drawn onto your grey Mi-Teintes paper. Gently round the chin area and draw the hair, face, neck and clothing.

2. When drawing the eyes (see Figs. 5a and 5e) it's very important to **draw the three angles** on both the top and bottom lids of the eyes and draw the curve over the top of those three angles after that. Only draw a part of the iris as some of it cannot be seen due to the top eyelid covering it (see insert Fig. 5a.) For more ideas on how to draw an eye see Figs. 5b, 5c, 5d and 5e.

3. Draw a basic outline for the nose; just draw the large ball and the nostrils at this stage (Figs. 5f, 5g.) Refer to your original photograph constantly for the correct shape and size of nose you are drawing. The shape of the area on the tip of the nose and nostrils are unique to everyone. Begin with a circle and then shape the circle according to the photograph you are working from.

4. Draw the construction drawing shapes and then the outline for the lips (see Figs. 5h and 5i.) Concentrate very carefully on the area between the top and bottom lip. This shape, which is often just a line with variety, will need careful consideration and finer work later, but just concentrate on placing the major angles here. Draw one half of the middle line first then the other. Make a little marker at the halfway point on the image and drawing.

www.DrawPJ.com

Step Four: Begin shading the features, starting with the eyes

Tip: before you start shading, its wise to know more about the underlying muscles in the face. You can learn more by reading anatomy books or researching online.

For the shading technique, use the chisel point preparation number 2 and 3 (for medium and small areas) making sure that the point is not as long as what we require for creating fine lines.

1. Add the extra rolls of skin around the eye lids and begin shading by carefully adding some charcoal to your page using the large flat area of the chisel point (see Fig. 6.) Shape the area using your putty eraser and cotton tip as well as adding more charcoal as needed (revisit your techniques number 2 and 3.)
2. Add eyebrows with a small amount of charcoal using the tip of your willow charcoal and the large flat part of the tip as needed, with a very gentle touch. This will help you to create realistic eyebrows. Go easy on drawing the individual hairs and concentrate more on shading the major tones, think in mass and tone rather than hairs.
3. Use a combination of smooth shading and the occasional short lines using the tip of the charcoal for the tiny hairs.
4. Don't draw everything you see, eyebrows shouldn't dominate the face, so try to keep them subtle. Less is best in this area.
5. Notice that the darkest level six areas are reserved for around the eye lid lines.
6. Complete the second eye and eye-brow.

Very important tips: Consider your putty eraser and your cotton bud (or paper stump) to be equally important as a drawing tool as the willow charcoal. You draw with your putty eraser and you draw with your paper stump and cotton bud. These tools can be used as though they are a pencil.

Remember to leave the highlight areas as the blank page. White Conté will be placed within these areas as the finishing touch later. Do not add the white Conté yet as it can become 'muddied' or over-worked and grey which is not an appealing look.

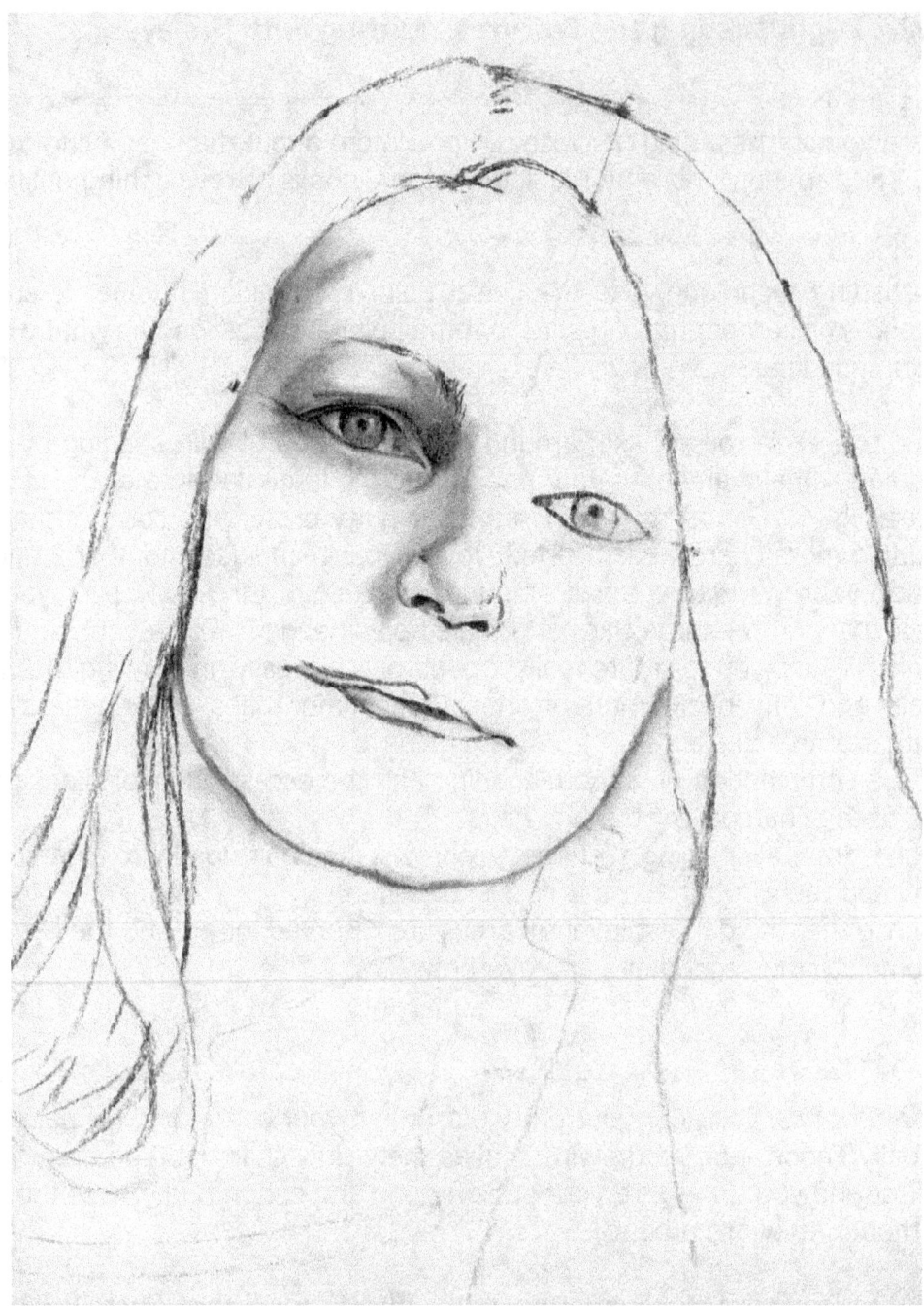

Fig. 6. Begin shading in the eye area

Step Five: Continue shading from the top of the hair

1. Shade some charcoal within the roots of the hair using the flat area and the tip of the chisel point on your willow charcoal stick as needed (see Fig. 7.) work by stroking in the direction of the hair out and away from the scalp. Also shade the hair and shadow areas around the forehead.
2. Shade the forehead a little then continue to travel down the face under the eye areas and around the cheeks.
3. Begin to work in the nose area (see Fig. 7) Continually refer to your original photograph and remember to squint so that you can see the details. Please refer back to your notes from the previous weeks of the course.

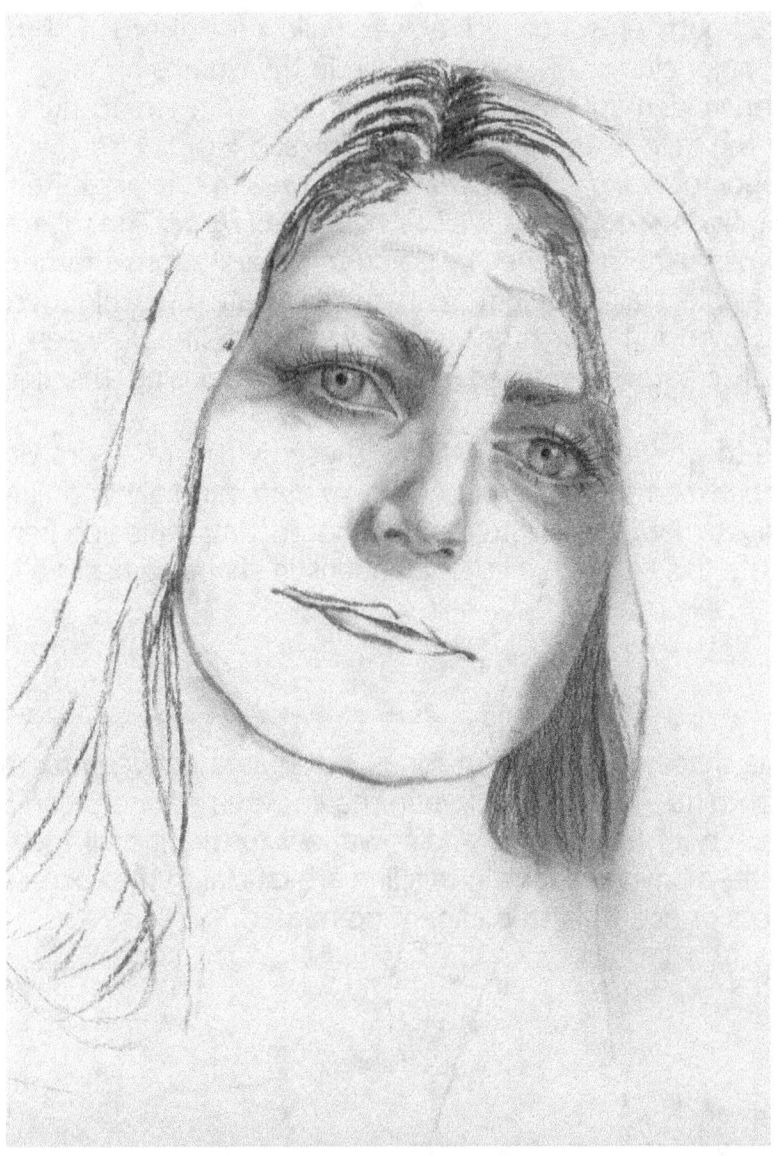

Fig. 7. Continue shading from the top of the hair

Step Six: Continue shading the hair then lips and cheek areas

It is important to keep moving around the portrait so that it has a unified-feel to the drawing as a whole. This will also help to prevent smudging your work by gradually working down from top to bottom.

1. You can go back to working in the hair area and draw in some major directional strokes *using your 2B charcoal pencil*. Read your notes from *week two* on hair to be reminded of how to draw hair.

2. Shade some charcoal within the darker shadow areas of the hair using the flat ellipse-shape of the chisel point on your medium sized willow charcoal stick (see Fig. 8.) Blend these areas using your paper stump and following the direction of the hair. Remove any areas in the hair that are highlighted using either your putty eraser or click eraser. Follow the direction of the hair and seek out any major clumps. Try to work within the clumps of hair.

3. Continue working your way across the face from left to right and shade the sides of the face in the cheek and chin (see Fig. 8.) You will find there is a combination of *hard edges and soft edges* in this area. Remember to seek out any *shadow edges* as well as *reflected light*. The reflected light shapes are very useful because they help you to separate forms rather than having to draw a single black outline. You can separate the chin from the neck for example, by using your putty eraser to draw a line between the two shapes which will create a reflected light area by exposing the lighter grey page underneath.

4. Continue to work on the lips refining these by first of all drawing the shape of the line between the top and bottom lip very carefully and slowly. Look at all the changes that occur. Note that it is not just a simple line here. Do your best to replicate this line with all the variations in shape as best you can (see insert Fig. 8.)

Tip: The various shapes and depth of tones in the area between the top and bottom lip are very important. This section (when the lips are not open) can be seen only as a line with a variety of tiny shapes adding variety to the line all the way along. The way you draw these tiny variations in this line are crucial to the success of the portrait gaining a likeness or not. This step cannot be hurried.

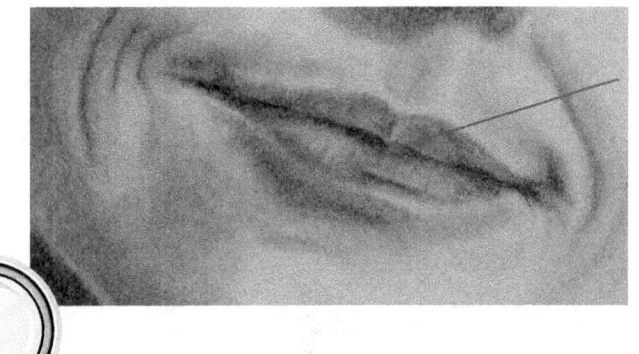

The area between the top and bottom lips is very important. Draw this area with great care and attention to detail.

Use your putty eraser to draw the line which separates the chin and neck area. This line is to indicate the reflected light area. Even if you can't see this reflected light in your photograph it is important to draw it as it helps your viewer to differentiate between the two areas; chin and neck.

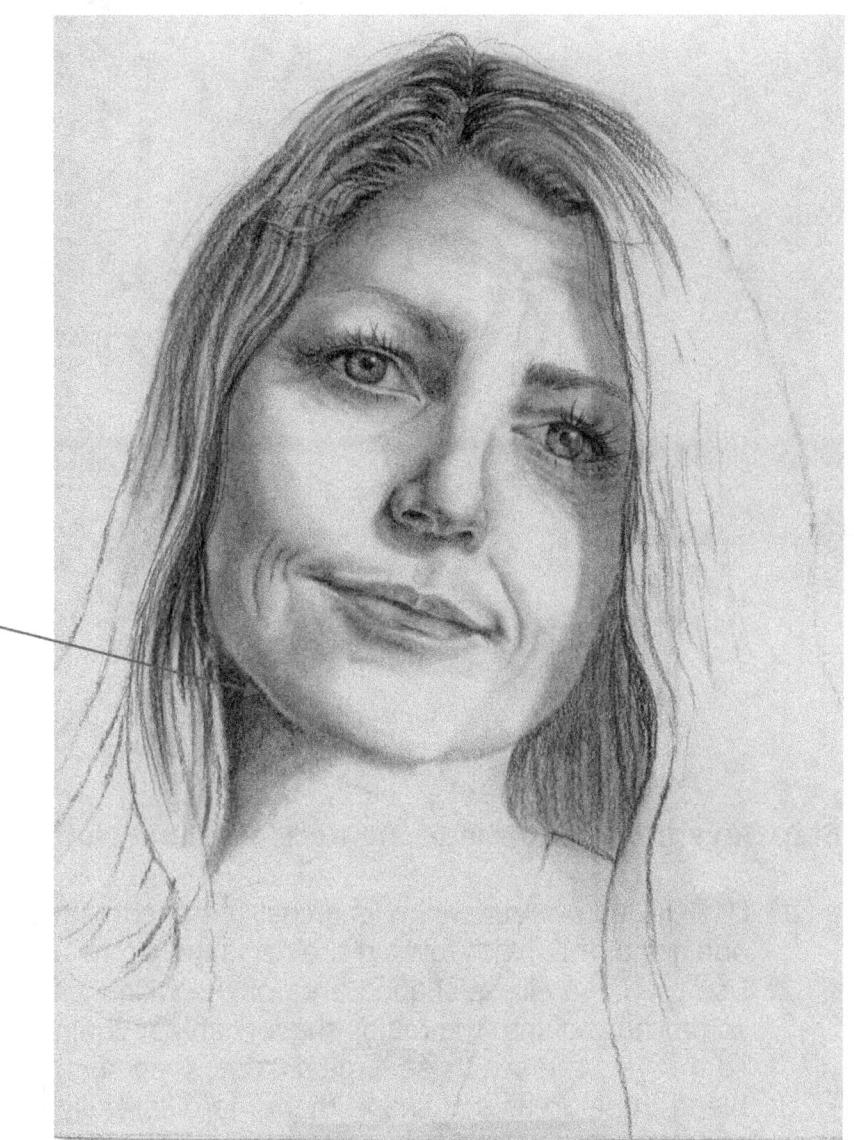

Fig. 8. Continue shading in the hair and the lips

www.DrawPJ.com

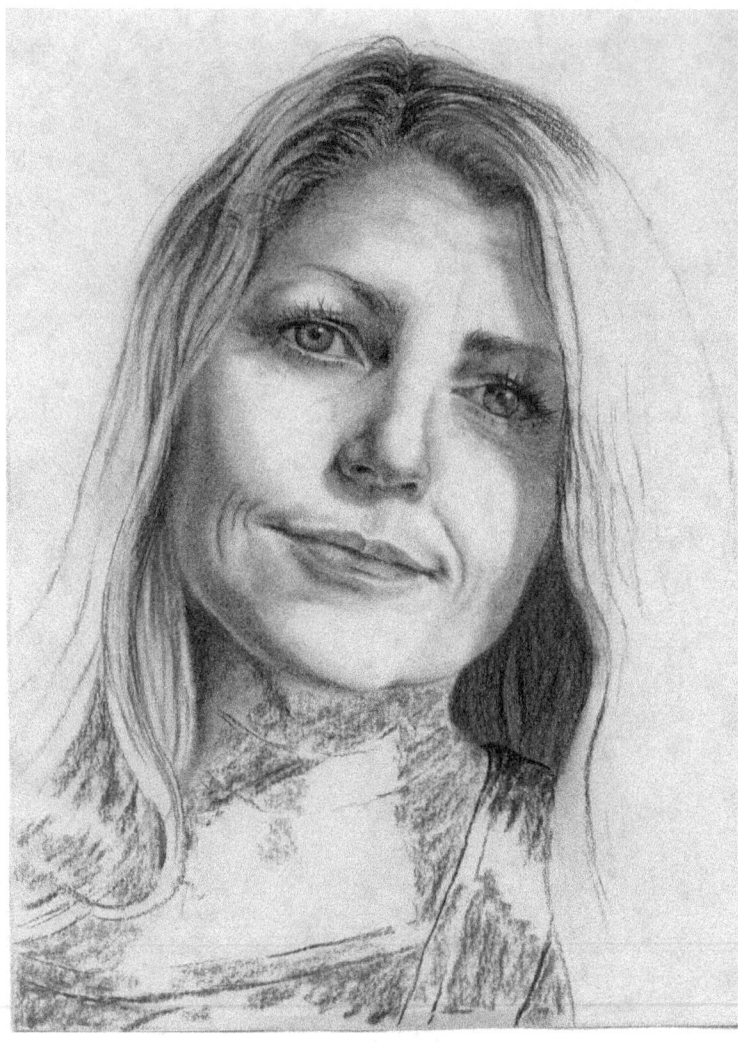

Fig. 9. Begin to shade the neck area and clothes

Step Seven: Begin to shade the neck area and clothes

1. Use the tip of your willow charcoal prepared with a chisel point to draw the outlines of the major folds in the neck and clothes (see Fig. 9.)
2. Use the large ellipse-shaped area of the willow charcoal stick to softly lay on some charcoal into the major shadow areas. Squint with your eyes half-closed so that you can see these large shadow shapes.
3. Blend these areas and shape them more carefully with your putty eraser and paper stump as you work your way from top to bottom in the neck and shirt area (see Fig. 10.)
4. Complete this area by adding more depth to the darker areas using your 2B charcoal pencil if necessary to gain a darker tone.
5. Continue shading the hair on the left side using your 2B charcoal pencil and erase any highlighted areas as necessary (see Fig. 10.)

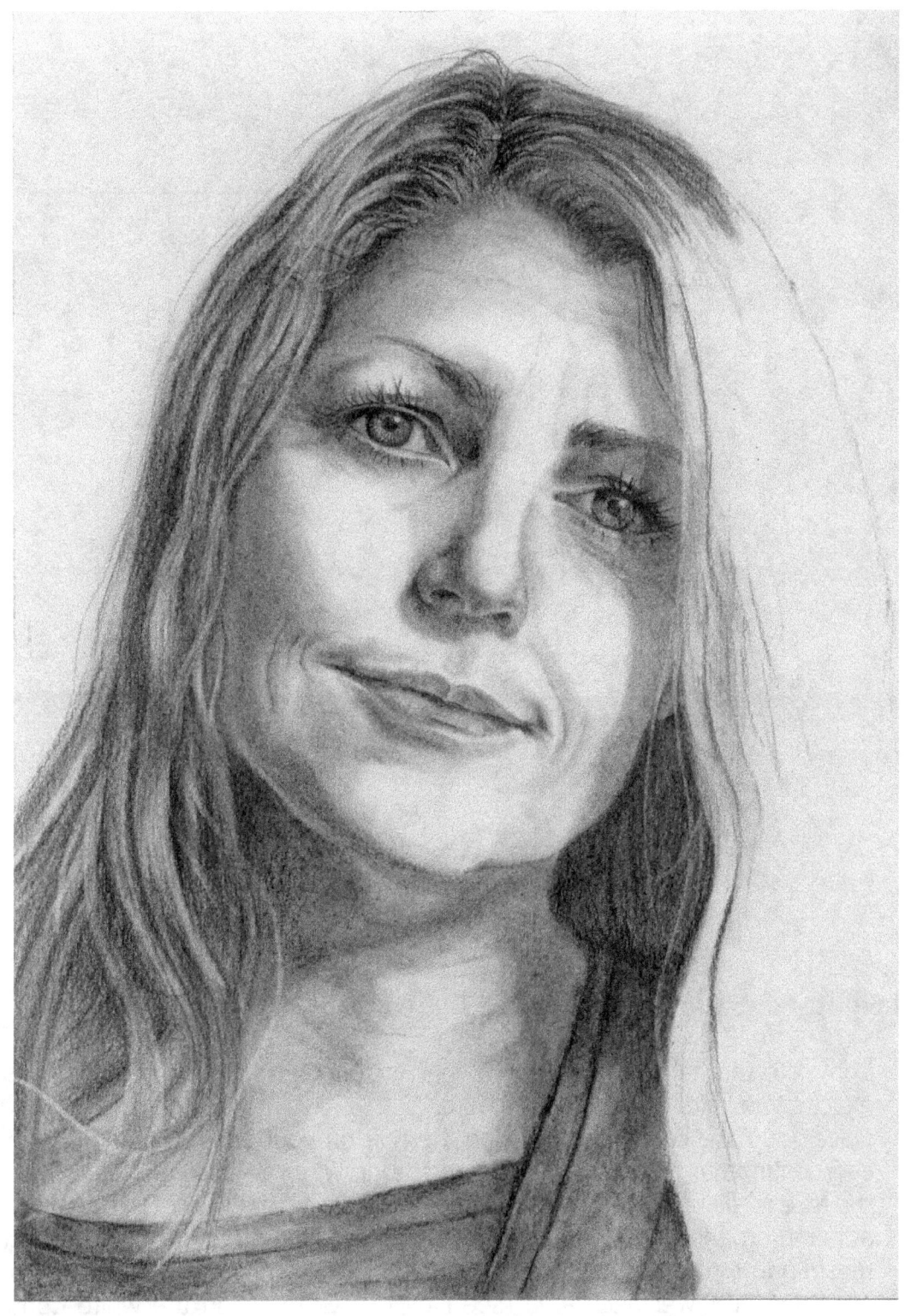

Fig. 10. Blend the neck area and work on the hair on the left side

www.DrawPJ.com

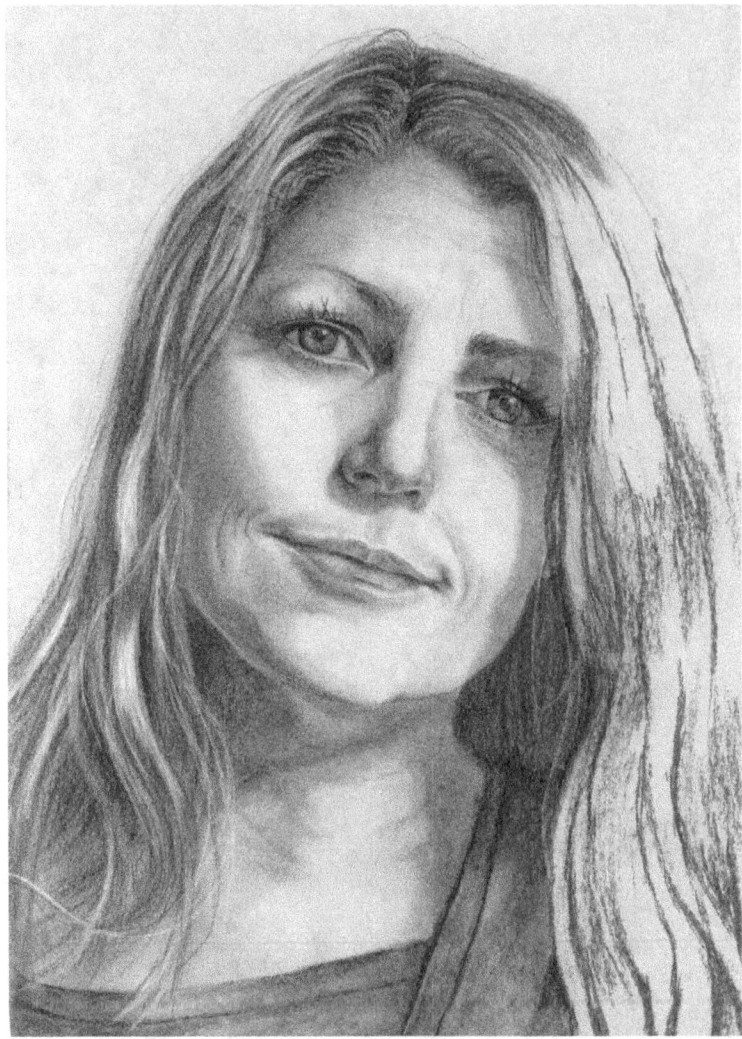

Fig. 11. Continue to work on the right side of the hair

Step Eight: Continue to work on the right side of the hair

1. Complete the hair by referring to your **week two notes** on hair as it is the exact same hairstyle as this one here.
2. Once you have completed drawing the hair on your portrait (see Fig. 12) you can continue to complete the rest of the drawing by adding white Conté to the face (see Fig. 13.) There are some major areas that white Conté is generally added on to the face. These areas protrude the most and therefore reflect the most light; forehead, eye-lids, bridge and tip of the nose, cheek-bones, bottom lip, chin and lower neck area (see Fig. 13.) Go easy on the white Conté for maximum effect. You don't have to shade the entire area that has been left as the blank page, just shade the Conté on within the middle of the area and follow the shape of the form.
3. With this final step in place your self-portrait is complete.

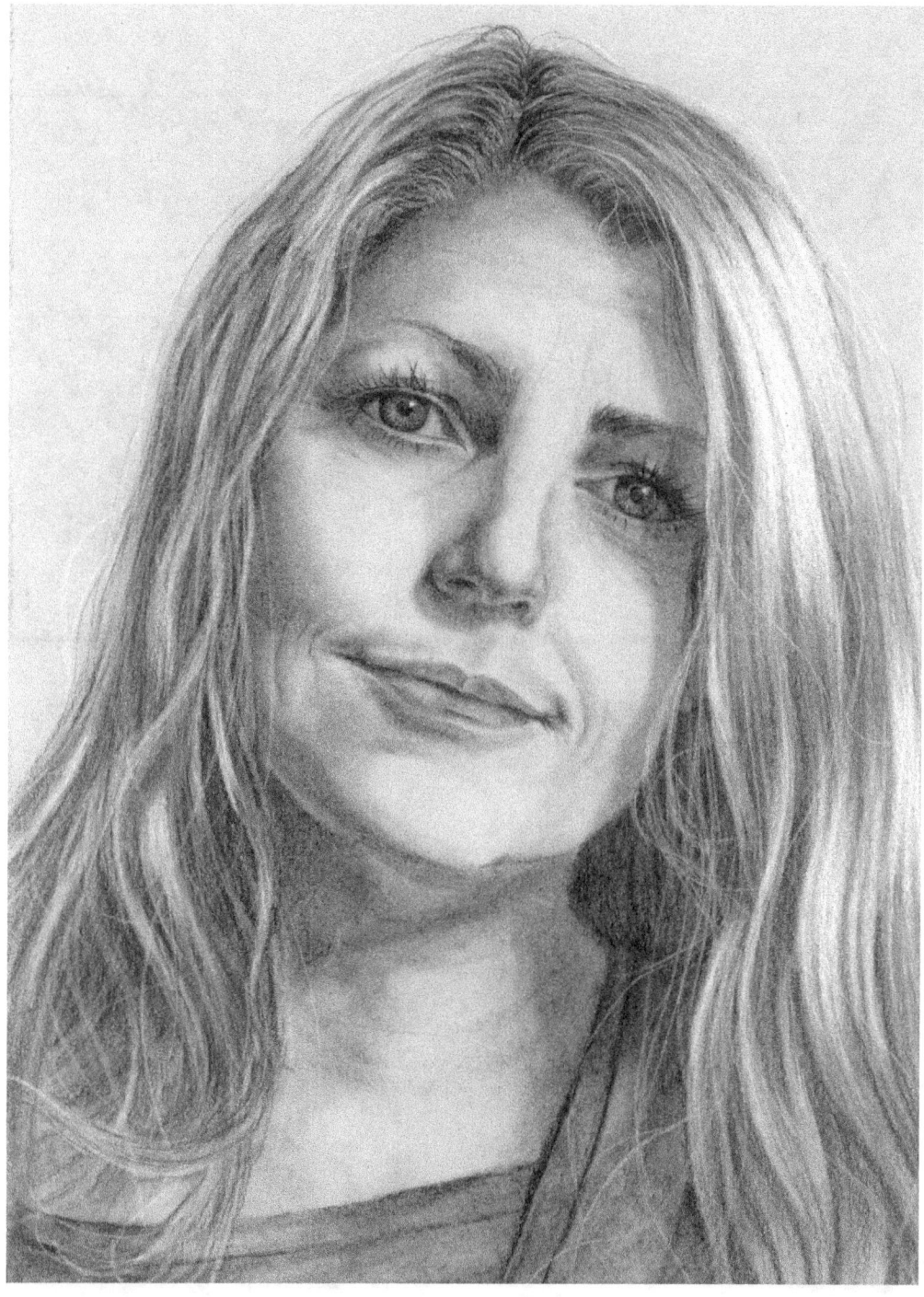

Fig. 12. Complete the hair using white Conté and white charcoal pencil

www.DrawPJ.com

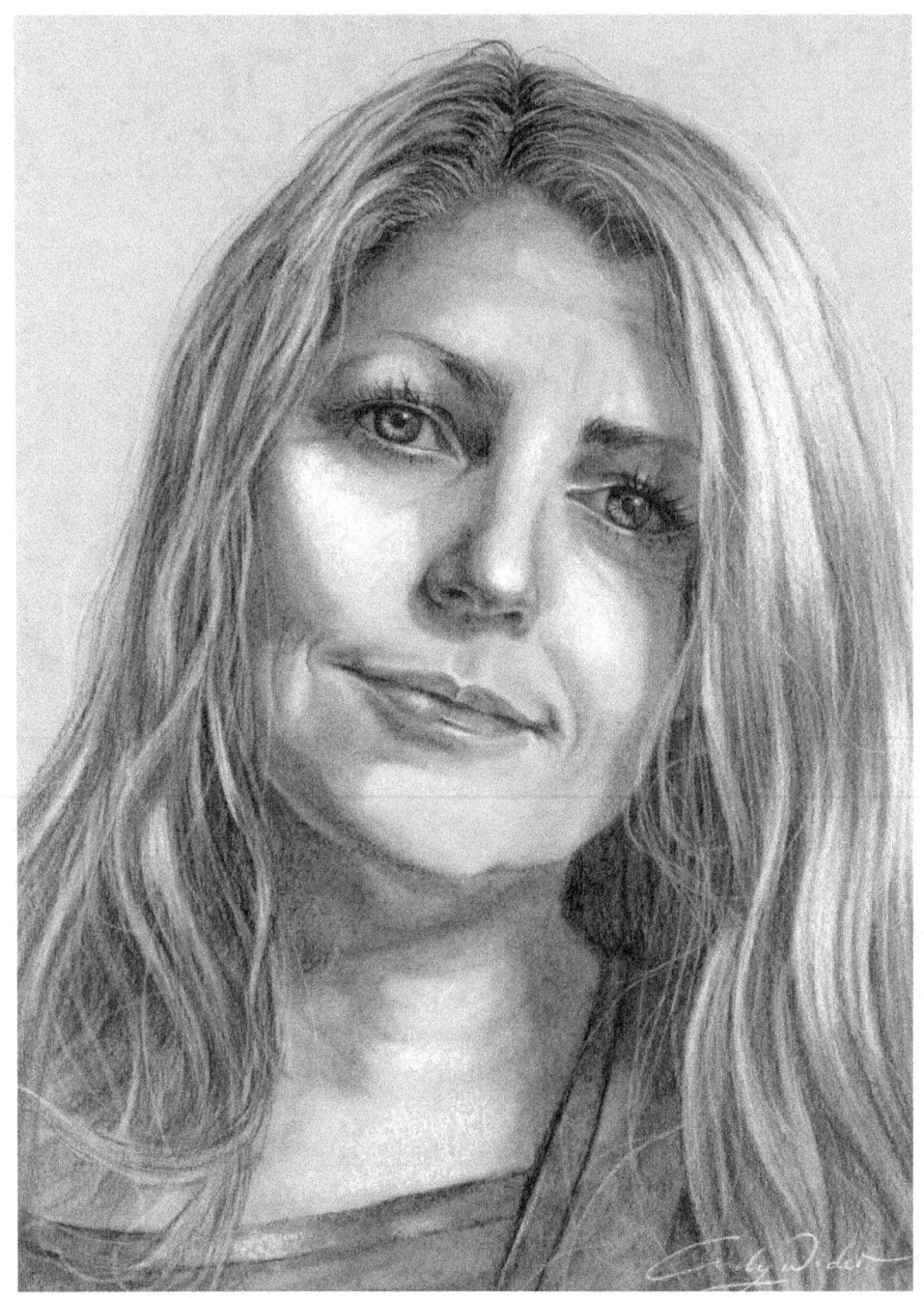

Fig. 13. The completed portrait 'Just me'

www.DrawPJ.com

Examples of Self Portraits by Previous Course Participants 'Before' and 'After' drawings:

Here are some examples of previous course participants' charcoal and white conté drawings of 'A Self Portrait.' These students have also studied the 'Complete Drawing and Painting Certificate Course' units; one, three and four (which includes this charcoal course as part of the unit 4 course). You are invited to email your completed portrait along with your pre-instruction drawing to me Cindy Wider cindy@drawpj.com to celebrate your success with this course.

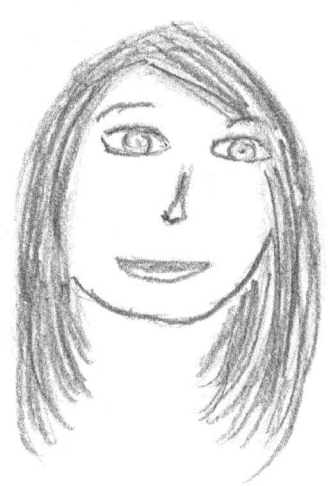

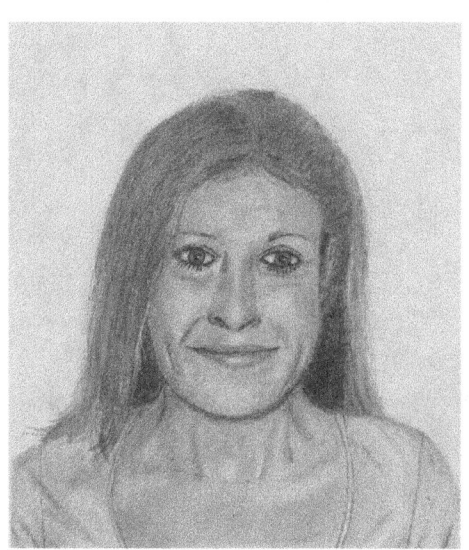

Before Drawing by katrina-coltzau   'After' Drawing by katrina-coltzau

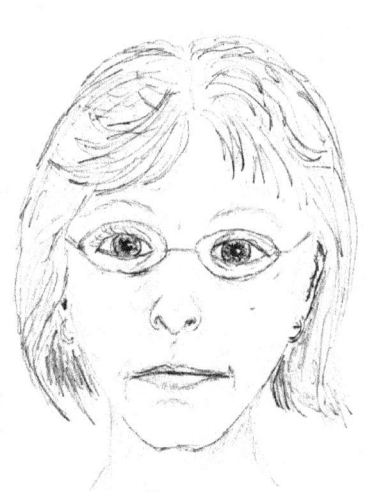

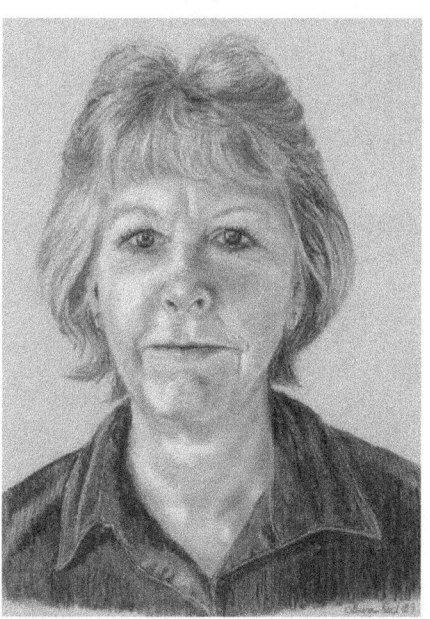

Before Drawing by Laura Rud   'After' Drawing by Laura Rud

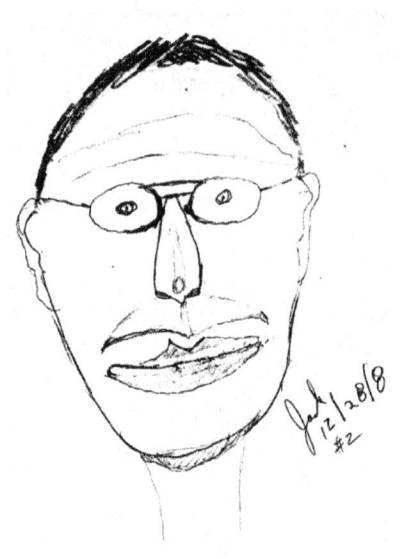

Before Drawing by Jack Gilbert

'After' Drawing by Jack Gilbert

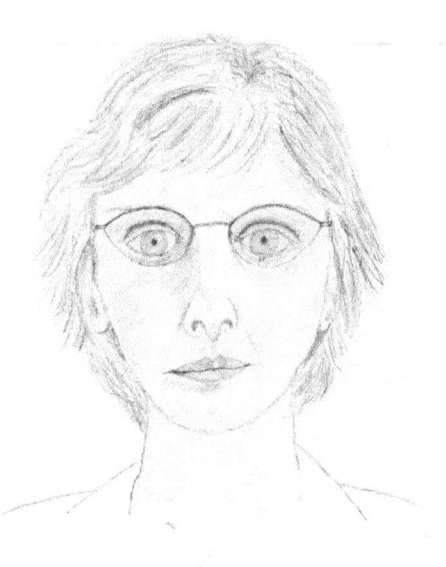

Before Drawing by Lisa F. Mac Donald

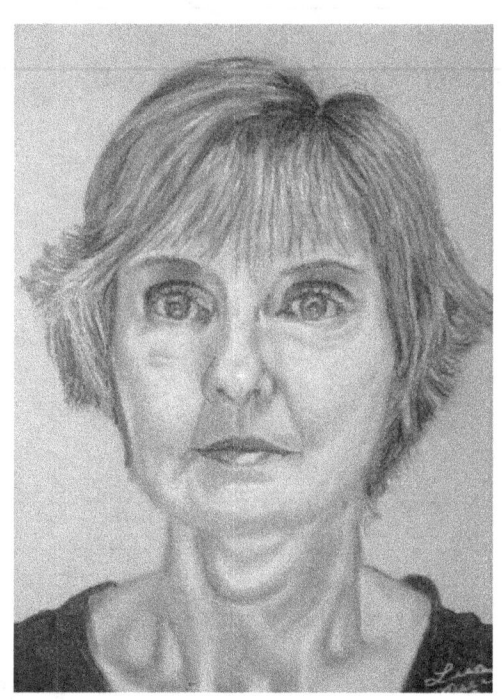

'After' Drawing by Lisa F. Mac Donald

Final Words

Among the many valued lessons that you might gain from creating your own self-portrait is the realisation that all human faces are really beautiful in their own way, including your own. Human faces are all just different and we need to ask ourselves the questions; "what is beauty anyhow? What measure do we compare beauty against?"

For example, when drawing any person (even someone you thought was truly beautiful,) you will soon discover some interesting things such as; their two ears might be different to one another. One ear could be higher or lower than the other. One eye lid might droop significantly more on one eye than the other and a nose often veers over to one side, however the person is still very attractive.

When we are drawing a likeness to a person, the differences that make us all unique are quite delicate and can sometimes vary simply by the width of even the thinnest charcoal line. By changing an angle, length or width of a line just the slightest bit can alter the entire look of a person.

Through this course, we have witnessed hundreds of people drawing their self-portraits over the years and many report the same amazing realisation and self-acceptance. Some are brought to tears as they stare at themselves for the very first time in the completed image. Most cannot believe what they have achieved through the creation of this drawing.

For some people the drawing doesn't gain a likeness until the final hour. You can probably expect this to happen to you too. Many people take their portraits on a journey of appearing like their mothers, fathers, grandparents, uncles, aunties, children or even grandchildren before they finally appear like themselves.

Continue and persevere with the creation of this drawing while speaking gentle encouraging words to yourself. Patience will be your most valuable personal characteristic here. Keep going even while your head tells you that you can't. Tell yourself, *"I can and I will."* Sometimes it is best not to show your drawing to others until your portrait is completely finished. This will give you a chance to discover all the little nuances for yourself as well as develop confidence along the way. Take regular breaks from your portrait and come back to visit often.

In summary, to create a self-portrait is a rewarding and liberating experience. I wish you all the best on this incredible journey of self-discovery. Remember that the *learning is in the process not the destination.* The destination is just an accumulation of all of your experiences along the journey.

Remember to 'Just show up at your table' and the rest will take care of itself! Have a fun day!

About the Author Cindy Wider

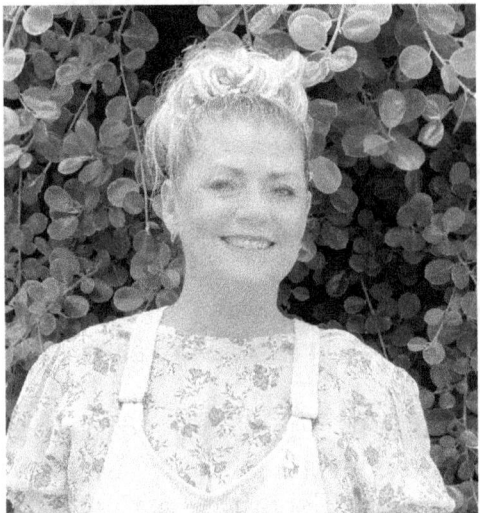

Cindy Wider lives in Cairns Far North Queensland Australia along with her husband Stuart, two teenage daughters and their much-loved pets; Jet the dog and Wednesday the cat.

She can be found most days in her studio, either online in CindysDrawingClub.com or at her art table creating the imagery for her up-coming children's picture book with the 'Cuddleecat Family and Friends.'

Cindy's entire career in the art industry spans over 31 years as a full-time professional educator, award-winning artist, author and illustrator.

As a mentor, and through her art education books, videos, magazine articles, TV appearances and more, Cindy has inspired tens of thousands of others to discover the wonderful world of drawing and colouring for themselves.

www.DrawPJ.com

www.ingramcontent.com/pod-product-compliance
Lightning Source LLC
Chambersburg PA
CBHW081503170526
45166CB00008B/2529